Some Microeconomics of Higher Education

Some Microeconomics of Higher Education

Economies of Scale

JAMES MAYNARD

UNIVERSITY OF NEBRASKA PRESS · LINCOLN

Publishers on the Plains
UNP

Copyright © 1971 by the University of Nebraska Press

All Rights Reserved

International Standard Book Number 0–8032–0792–1

Library of Congress Catalog Card Number 76–139371

Manufactured in the United States of America

To My Wife, Jeanne

Contents

Preface   xiii

Introduction   1

Why the Economist's Neglect of the Microeconomics
of Higher Education?   6
Purpose of This Study   11

1. *An Overview of American Higher Education*   12

Higher Education Defined   12
Macroeconomic Characteristics of American Higher
Education   15
Microeconomic Characteristics of American Higher
Education   23
Summary   40

2. *The Theory of Long-Run Costs in Higher Education: Some
Preliminary Matters*   43

Long-Run Average Costs for the Firm   44
Microeconomic Theory and Higher Education   47
Costs of IHL: Some Broad Influences   54
The Educational Activities of IHL: A Description   58
Summary   61

3. *Expenditures for the Core Functions of the Institutions of
Higher Learning*   64

Plant Maintenance and Operation   65
Libraries   70

Organized Activities Relating to Instruction   71
General Administration, General Expense, and Student
   Services   72
Instruction and Departmental Research   75
Total Educational and General Activities   83
Summary   84

4. *An Empirical Test of the Theoretical Long-Run Cost Function
for Institutions of Higher Learning*   88

Rationale and Composition of the Study   88
Estimation of a General IHL Long-Run Cost Function   94
Relevance of the Four-Year IHL Long-Run Cost
   Function for Private Schools   107
Behavior of Separate Educational and General Activities   112
Summary   113

5. *Some Concluding Observations*   116

Reconciliation with Russell and Reeves and the
   Durability of the General Function   116
Implications of the Four-Year IHL Long-Run Cost
   Function for Contemporary Higher Education   119
Summary   129

*Appendix A: Peripheral Activities of Institutions of Higher
Learning*   133

Organized Research and Other Sponsored Programs   133
Extension and Public Service   136
Summary   137

*Appendix B: The Statistical Derivation of the Four-Year IHL
Long-Run Cost Function*   139

IHL Composition of the Study   139

Computation of the Intermediate Long-Run Cost
  Functions   146
Development of the Four-Year IHL Long-Run Cost
  Function   150
Summary   155

Appendix C: A Review of the Literature   158

The North Central Association Study   158
The Study of Church-Related Liberal Arts Colleges   162
Summary   164

Appendix D: Miscellaneous Cross-Section Functions   165

Cost Functions for Educational and General Activities   165
Total Cost Functions for Junior Colleges   171
Summary   173

Bibliography   175

Index   181

List of Figures

1.1 Percentage Distribution, Public and Private Universities, All Resident Students, Fall, 1967 26

1.2 Percentage Distribution, Public and Private Four-Year Colleges, All Resident Students, Fall, 1967 27

1.3 Percentage Distribution, Public and Private Junior Colleges, All Resident Students, Fall, 1967 28

3.1 Envelope Diagram of Actual Short-Run and Theoretical Long-Run Functions Relating Real Per-Student Institutional Cost and Size of Institution 81

4.1 Intermediate Cost Functions, Thirteen Subject States 97

4.2 The Four-Year IHL Long-Run Cost Function, Assuming an Ordinate Intercept of $1,500 100

4.3 Total Cost Function 102

4.4 Marginal Cost Function 103

B.1 Scatter Diagram, Paired r^2 and b Values, Thirteen Intermediate Functions 152

B.2 Scatter Diagram, Paired b and c Values, Thirteen Intermediate Functions 154

C.1 Enrollment and Educational Expenditure per Student for Institutions in Lowest Quality Grouping 161

List of Tables

1.1 Total Employment of Professional Persons, All Higher Education, Selected Years, Fall, 1955–63   16

1.2 Total Degree-Credit Enrollments, All Higher Education, Selected Years, Fall, 1955–67   18

1.3 Total Expenditures, All Higher Education, Selected Years, 1940–64, in Millions of Dollars   21

1.4 Total Institutions, Selected Years, 1961–67   23

1.5 Size Distribution, All Public Institutions, 1967   24

1.6 Size Distribution, All Private Institutions, 1967   25

1.7 Summary Microeconomic Statistics, All IHL, 1957–58 and 1963–64, Percent Change   37

1.8 Total Current Revenues and Expenditures: Percentage Analysis, All IHL, 1957–58, 1961–62, and 1963–64   39

2.1 Average Wage and Salary Personal Income, All Employees in Services and State and Local Government, by Regions, 1966   56

2.2 Per Capita Personal Income and Percent of IHL with Mean Faculty Salary in Excess of National Average, by Regions, 1968   57

3.1 Rank-Order Correlation Results: Gross Academic Building Space on Fall Head Counts, Illinois IHL, 1965   67

4.1 Formulas for Staffing State-Controlled Four-Year IHL: Thirteen Subject States, 1967–68   93

4.2 Intermediate Average-Cost Functions: Thirteen Subject States   96

4.3 The Four-Year IHL Long-Run Cost Function, Assuming an Ordinate Intercept of $1,500 in 1967–68 Dollars 99

4.4 Rank-Order Correlation Coefficients: Ratio of Graduate to Undergraduate FTE Students on Total FTE Students, Thirteen Subject States 106

4.5 Percentage Distribution: Bachelor's Degrees Conferred in Six Major Fields, All IHL, 1965–66 108

4.6 Difference-in-Means Test Results: Student-Personnel Ratios, Public and Private Four-Year IHL, Fall, 1966 110

4.7 Difference-in-Means Test Results: Student-Teacher Ratios, Public and Private Four-Year IHL, Fall, 1967 111

5.1 All Universities and Four-Year Teachers and Liberal Arts Colleges, by FTE Students, Fall, 1967 120

B.1 Ratio, Highest to Lowest Average Institutional Full-Time Faculty Salary, Public and Private: Subject States, 1967–68 143

B.2 Indices and Coefficients of Determination, Parabolic and Linear Functions, and Sign of Slope Coefficient for Linear Function 149

D.1 Intermediate States, Cost Functions for Separate Activities: Index of Determination, Constants, and Minimum Cost Level of FTE Students 167

D.2 Least-Squares Parabolic Functions: Indices of Determination and Constants, Two Intermediate States 172

Preface

Like knowledge and learning, positive and normative economics are both related and different; however, the relation is more interesting than the difference. In both cases the relation is such that the former must precede the latter in time. There must be knowledge before there can be learning, and there must be some idea of what the nature of economic phenomena is before anything very meaningful can be said, or done, about what ought to be the nature of the same phenomena. This is particularly germane now, for today normative economics is much the vogue. However, some practitioners seem to have forgotten the basic truth of the observation that first must come the positive if the normative is to be endowed with analytical and substantive meaning.

I think a case can be made for the proposition that normative statements have outpaced positive analysis when the microeconomics of higher education is considered. There is a wealth of statistical data pertinent to current and past operations of colleges and universities. And literally every educator has an opinion on how resources should be divided between (1) higher education and the rest of society and (2) his institution and others. But an exhaustive search will fail to uncover a definitive body of positive economic theory concerning the microeconomics of higher education, which would be the logical extension of the analysis from accumulation of copious quantities of statistical data and would serve as the standard upon which normative statements could be based.

This book is an attempt to add something to a woefully sparse body of positive microeconomic theory concerning

American higher education. It is not directly intended to be normative or prescriptive, although, as with any body of positive economic theory, the potential for normative application exists. The book is, most specifically, an attempt to discern and summarize the existing nature of some microeconomic characteristics of a significant portion of American higher education. I think the attempt is successful.

I would here like to express my profound appreciation to the hundreds of school officials and executives of governing boards and coordinating councils for their willingness to take time from crowded schedules to supply basic data, without which this study would have been impossible. This is all the more significant when it is considered that much of the data was either confidential in nature or not generally intended for circulation to other than concerned decision makers. I would also like to express my gratitude to my wife, Jeanne. Without her encouragement, patience, and yeoman performance on the typewriter and calculator, the project would have been immensely more difficult. Finally, as tradition dictates, I accept full responsibility for all analyses and conclusions contained herein, both express and implied.

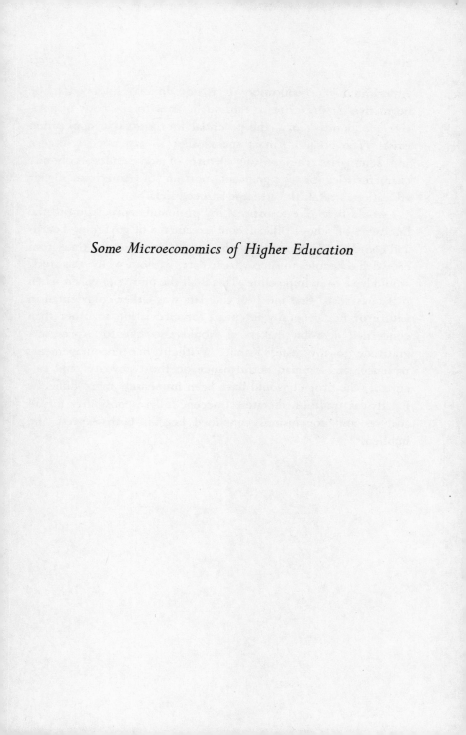

Some Microeconomics of Higher Education

Introduction

Recent years have seen a pronounced increase in the attention devoted to higher education by economists acting in their professional capacity. This attention has not been limited to higher education, but has included primary and secondary schooling, vocational education, and other kinds of formal instruction for resident students. The increased attention paid education by economists prompted Dr. Allan M. Cartter facetiously to warn the 1964 annual meeting of the American Economics Association as follows:

> In the four short years since [the presidential address by Professor Theordore Schultz to the 1960 annual meeting of the AEA] the economics of education has become a popular enough subject to run the danger now of becoming fashionable.[1]

The invitation extended to Dr. Cartter, one of the nation's experts on the economic problems of colleges and universities, to address the assemblage of economists lends credence to the above observation that the economics of higher education is becoming an increasingly "legitimate" area of interest for economists. And perhaps the most signal recognition of the acceptance of higher education within the economist's discipline is the inclusion, in a book of readings designed to augment a new economic principles textbook, of an article entitled "The Economics of Higher Education."[2]

1. Allan M. Cartter, "Economics of the University," *Papers and Proceedings, 77th Annual Meeting, American Economics Association* 55, no. 2 (1965): 485.

2. Allan M. Cartter, "The Economics of Higher Education," in *Contemporary Economic Issues*, ed. Neil W. Chamberlain (Homewood, Ill.: Richard D. Irwin, 1969), pp. 145–84.

Certainly, the economist's concern with higher education, as something more than the institution which trained him and provides a means of personal livelihood, is relatively recent (with the exception of Professor Seymour Harris's studies). This late-blooming interest in higher education may well be due to two factors: one, the abatement of a kind of inhibition about the pursuit of the subject, the other, a stimulating effect which is the product of a few scholars' viewing education in a different light.

In the past forty years, economists have devoted a great deal of attention to studying—and seeking to understand—the macroeconomic phenomena of the industrial, market economy. Such concern was proper and socially responsible because the problems of unemployment, prices, economic development, and economic growth were uppermost in the collective minds of most Western nations. However, concentration in one area simply did not leave much time for many economists to devote more than sporadic interest to such things as the theory of the conglomerate firm, rational decision making for the provision of defense for the nation, or the economics of education. But a complex combination of influences has today resulted in some relative shift in economists' attention away from the above mentioned macroeconomic problems of the 1930–60 era, and toward what seem to be different kinds of problems in the post-1960 period. This is not to suggest that economists have abandoned the study of what could now be called traditional macroeconomic phenomena; however, it does appear that they are increasingly turning their thoughts to the study of the quality of economic life and the nature of social institutions which have heretofore escaped much scrutiny.

The other factor which has likely contributed to economists' increased professional interest in higher education is the recent work of a few economists spotlighting education as a strategic element in the economic growth process of a modern, industrial economy.[3] Once education, especially higher education, was seen as more than just "a means of building character and training for leadership in public affairs—army, church, and state,"[4] and instead, an influence which "from 1929 to 1957 . . . raised the average quality of labor [in the United States] by 29.6 percent, or at an average annual rate of 0.93 percent,"[5] economists were bound to become more interested.

At this point it is well to describe specifically what one pursues when studying the economics of higher education. Basically, the economics of higher education is not unlike the economics of most other industries, with the important exception that one is a little more reverent when studying the former. For as Gordon Ray states, "Higher education, like medicine, law, and the operation of our Armed Forces is only incidentally an 'economic activity.'"[6] Notwithstanding this difference, the economics of higher education involves (1) study of the nature of and influences on the allocation of resources, in the aggregate, between the higher education industry and the rest of the economy, with an attempt to discern the societal implications of alternative quantitative allocations—this could be called the *macro*economics of higher education and (2) study of conditions within the industry such as entry and exit of new institutions or other producing entities, the state of technology, the nature of pricing the product(s) and the influence of these pricing

3. See Gary S. Becker, *Human Capital* (New York: National Bureau of Economic Research, 1964); Edward F. Denison, *The Sources of Economic Growth and the Alternatives before Us* (New York: Committee for Economic Development, 1962); and Theordore W. Schultz, *The Economic Value of Education* (New York, Columbia University Press, 1963).

4. Cartter, "Economics of Higher Education," p. 145.

5. Denison, *Sources of Economic Growth*, p. 73.

6. Gordon N. Ray, "Conflict and Cooperation in American Higher Education," in *Financing Higher Education: 1960–70*, ed. Dexter M. Keezer (New York: McGraw-Hill, 1959), p. 104.

practices on both the quantity and quality of product(s), and conditions affecting the structure and level of costs—these would constitute the *micro*economics of higher education.

The recent attention given higher education by economists falls under the heading of the macroeconomics of higher education. In turn, this attention has seen two rather distinct phases. First, from about the mid-1950s until the emergence of Denison's work in 1962, the study of the macroeconomics of higher education involved economists assisting college administrators and trustees, government officials, and others in search of a solution to the following question: Where was America to find the increased resources necessary for higher education in the 1960s? These increased requirements seemed to be due to two unrelated phenomena, namely, the challenge to the quality of American education manifested in Sputnik and the increased quantity of higher education necessitated by the dramatic rise in birth rates during the 1940s. This phase in the study of the macroeconomics of higher education produced a prodigious number of special conferences and seminars, as well as a significant body of literature.[7] The conclusions that emerged from this phase can be summarized in the following statement:

> In short, the essence of this nation's educational problem is that we have allowed a potentially disastrous educational lag to develop, a gap between our mounting educational requirements on the one side and our educational effort and performance on the other. . . . The central task for the United States, therefore, is to close this educational gap and keep it closed.[8]

The means of raising additional revenue were debated at length (that is, whether to increase student fees or to increase contribu-

7. See Seymour E. Harris, ed., *Higher Education in the United States: The Economic Problems* (Cambridge, Mass.: Harvard University Press, 1960) and Dexter M. Keezer, ed., *Financing Higher Education*.

8. Philip H. Coombs, "An Economist's Overview of Higher Education," in *Financing Higher Education*, ed. Keezer, p. 17.

tions from public coffers and private philanthropy). The substantial increase in revenues which most colleges and universities enjoyed in the 1960s came primarily from an increase in the charges to students and greater financial participation by all levels of government, especially the state governments.

The other phase in the study of the macroeconomics of higher education began about 1962 with the publication of Denison's work which stands as a landmark.[9] This phase has seen attention centered on the causal relationships between education and such macroeconomic phenomena as economic growth and development. Summarizing the impact of many specific, positive contributions that increased and intensified education can make to the economic growth and development process, Giuseppe Papi writes as follows:

> All these results follow from the employment of increasingly better educated and trained personnel in productive undertakings; and—even though the results become apparent only in the long run and are, therefore, hard to predict with precision—they reduce risks and costs. In other words they lead to economies, some "internal," but all eventually to the advantage of production.[10]

However, the issues described previously and classified under the subject heading of the microeconomics of higher education have not received a level of attention from economists comparable to that devoted to macroeconomic problems. In the words of Cartter, "We are at last developing a macroeconomic view of education, but we have not even begun to develop a counterpart view of education analogous to the theory of the firm."[11] More

9. Denison, *Sources of Economic Growth.*

10. Giuseppe U. Papi, "General Problems of the Economics of Education," in *The Economics of Education: Proceedings of a Conference Held by the International Economics Association*, eds. E. Austin G. Robinson and John E. Vaizey (New York: St. Martin's Press, 1966), p. 3.

11. Cartter, "Economics of the University," p. 489.

recently, an economist chastised his colleagues for their neglect of the microeconomics of higher education.

> Research conducted by economists on education as an investment in human beings has produced a growing literature on the "economics of education." Such subjects as measuring the returns to human investment, alternative means of financing education, and methods of easing shortages of teachers and plant have received considerable attention. Few economists, however, have taken a hard analytical look at education as an industry or at an educational institution as a firm.[12]

Although the microeconomics of higher education have been studied little by economists, the subject has not gone unattended by everyone. Indeed, college and university business and budget officers, state legislators, governors, and financial officials of state legislative and executive branches have devoted a great deal of time and thought to the microeconomic problems of education, especially higher education. Much of this work has not been appreciated by the academic community because it was often unpublished, sometimes lacked analytical rigor, and typically pertained to specific—rather than general—phenomena. But of interest here is the neglect of the microeconomics of higher education by economists, especially by those within the very institutions of interest; and it is to the reasons for this neglect that we now turn.

Why the Economist's Neglect of the Microeconomics of Higher Education?

The economist's neglect of the microeconomics of higher education has been noticed by those who are most concerned with

---

12. Melvin Lurie, "Toward a Survey of Faculty-Turnover Rates," *Journal of Higher Education* 38, no. 7 (October 1966): 389.

these economic problems in the real world. This section summarizes what seem to be the most significant reasons for this neglect. Bernard Sliger attributes it to (1) economists not being invited to lend their talents to the problems and (2) the fact that higher education presents an area of activity not easily analyzed by traditional economic concepts and tools.[13] Sliger's summary, however, leaves more questions than answers.

It is true that councils of war on the economics of higher education have tended to exclude economists, as well as other teaching faculty. This is well illustrated by the composition of the Commission on Financing Higher Education, sponsored by the Association of American Universities in 1949–52, and created to undertake a comprehensive analysis of the financial state and future of American higher education. This body was made up of two lawyers, two industrialists, seven men who were either college presidents or provosts, and one member of unidentified vocation. The reasons for the exclusion of teaching faculty are of more interest than just the fact of exclusion.

Cartter, as usual, has ideas about this conspicuous absence of teaching faculty from the important deliberations concerning higher education's problems and policies. He first notes that, especially in the case of economists, this exclusion has not been entirely without some negative assistance from economists themselves.

> Until very recently economists have . . . treated the university as sacrosanct and have spent their energies looking out through its windows at the rest of the world instead of viewing their own natural habitat. Perhaps fearing that a closer look would reveal an Augean Stable, they have spent thousands of man-years analyzing the behavior of business firms, financial entities, governments, households, trade unions, entrepreneurs, and most any other

13. Bernard F. Sliger, "Some Economic Aspects of Higher Education," *Educational Record* 42, no. 1 (January 1961): 62.

variety of institution and have scarcely given a thought to that one with which they are most closely and dependently connected.[14]

However, Cartter notes several positive difficulties an economist (or any other academician) might have if he attempted to study the microeconomics of higher education.

1. Academicians generally feel that the public understands little about the university, and that a little public knowledge could be of more danger to the structure of the University than no public knowledge at all; thus, the loyal and responsible member of the academic community is likely not to care to disseminate information about the microeconomics of higher education, and he does not, therefore, spend much time researching it.

2. To study the university as an economic institution might invite the application of "business" principles and procedures, to the detriment of the spirit of the university.

3. University administrators feel, by and large, that such economic matters as institutional finance and teaching loads are simply none of the faculty's business. This occurs when either administrators view themselves as employers, with the faculty as employees, or when the administration views itself as the mediator between faculty and governing boards.

4. Existing data on educational institutions are closely held and generally poor.[15]

The reasons suggested for academicians in general, and economists in particular, not studying the university as an economic entity are formidable enough in themselves. However, some go beyond the suggestions of Sliger and Cartter and hold that school administrators fear economists delving into the economics of the institution, and that this fear results in active opposition to such research. According to Alice Rivlin,

14. Cartter, "Economics of the University," pp. 481–82.
15. Ibid., pp. 482–83.

Some research in the economics of education—especially attempts to compute rates of return on investment in education or consideration of costs of alternative teaching methods—has met with protests from educators. The protests have been directed not so much against the methods and conclusions of the economists, *but against the whole idea of doing this kind of research*. Education, say some educators, is far too precious to be compared in crass money terms with the ordinary commodities and services. . . . Not all educators take such extreme positions, but even those who do not are often fearful that if economists are turned loose on educational problems they will recommend cheaper methods of doing things even though these methods produce inferior results. . . . Or they imagine economists estimating that the rate of return to an individual on investment in a college education is lower than on other investments (a conclusion not supported by any evidence so far) and advising that fewer students be sent to college—without considering the cultural and spiritual values of education to the individual or the benefits of his education to others besides himself.[16] [Emphasis added.]

Considering what Sliger, Cartter, and Rivlin have to say, the following picture seems to emerge:

1. Academicians, especially economists, have not studied the university as a producing entity, although the latter have devoted a little attention to some of the macroeconomic problems of higher education.
2. Even in the area of the macroeconomics of higher education, economists have met resistance from administrators who fear the economists' research might reveal higher education as an unsound investment at the margin for some persons, or unsound for society at the margin, given some present high level of college attendance.

16. Alice M. Rivlin, "Research in the Economics of Higher Education: Progress and Problems," in *Economics of Higher Education*, ed. Selma J. Mushkin (Washington, D.C.: GPO, 1962), p. 358.

3. However, the real neglect by economists has been of what can be called the microeconomics of higher education, and here there are both negative and positive influences at work. On the one hand, economists, as members of the academic community, fear public reaction to the revelation of anything about the operation of the institution that seems "unbusiness-like" to the layman. On the other hand, college and university administrators do not accept easily the idea of teaching faculty—economists or not—delving into institutional records which are, at best, poor. Many of these administrators also fear the results of research which might suggest that less expensive methods of pedagogy would be appropriate, such fear being either of the failure of the researchers to give sufficient weight to intangible (but extremely important) elements indigenous to present methods of instruction, or of the suggestions per se.

The author would like to here posit two other reasons why the economist has been negligent of the microeconomics of higher education. First, as mentioned above, until recently the economist has been absorbed in the problems of the classical national economy, especially to the extent that he could recommend measures for the avoidance and solution of such things as business cycle unemployment, inflation, and a lagging growth rate. These problems seem a little more susceptible to technical solutions now than was the case even ten years ago (although formidable political rigidities to the imposition of some of these solutions still persist), and many able economists have just recently felt free to devote some attention to such matters as higher education. Second, a significant portion of American higher education (about two-thirds of all students) is under the province of state and local governments, and economists have never demonstrated much inclination to study the economics of these levels of government. Perhaps this is because state and local governments are generally held to be devoid of characteristics susceptible to systematic analysis, and what state and local governments do is mostly explained by the vagaries of local, crude politics.

Undoubtedly, there are other reasons for the neglect of the microeconomics of higher education by economists. Perhaps most of this neglect can be traced to the following observation: "To those who prefer to think of education in terms of ideas and individual human beings, the money measurement of educational effort may seem somewhat abstract if not repulsive."[17] Whatever the reasons for economists' neglect of the microeconomics of higher education, the important fact is that it has been neglected.

Purpose of This Study

The general purpose of the remainder of this study will be to examine some microeconomic phenomena of American higher education. To accomplish this purpose, it will be necessary to (1) identify influences on the costs of a four-year undergraduate education among schools of various types and sizes; (2) relate the differences in per-student costs, attributable solely to differences in the size of the institution, to the economic principle of economics of scale; and (3) quantify the functional relationship between the size of the school and cost per student.

In effect this study will bring together (1) a basic tool of microeconomic analysis (the family of long-run cost functions) and (2) the higher education industry. This will be a step toward developing a microeconomic model of the institution of higher learning, a model that is now nonexistent.

17. Friedrich Edding, "Expenditure on Education: Statistics and Comments," in *Economics of Education*, eds. Robinson and Vaizey, p. 24.

An Overview of
American Higher Education

This initial chapter provides a broad, somewhat statistical look at American higher education in the present and near past. The first section defines higher education for analytical purposes and delineates the sundry types of institutions. It is followed by a summary macroanalysis of American higher education, concentrating on recent levels and trends in aggregate phenomena and relating these to national macroeconomic variables. The final section is devoted to selected microeconomic statistical data pertinent to higher education, and also describes common institutional practices which can be classified under this heading.

Higher Education Defined

The term *higher education* is not normally understood to be synonymous with "all post–secondary school formal education." Especially when one pursues statistical analysis, the federal government's definition of higher education is usually accepted, and it includes most of what one would likely include when discussing this segment of American formal education. The United States Department of Health, Education, and Welfare has established criteria to be met by institutions prior to their designation as institutions of higher education. These criteria, one of which must be met by the school before its identification as an institution of higher education, are

1. Actual accreditation by a nationally recognized accrediting body

2. Attainment of the status of preaccreditation whereby there is reasonable assurance that accreditation by a nationally recognized accrediting body is forthcoming

3. Acceptance of its credits, as equal to those from accredited institutions, by at least three accredited institutions

4. Approval by a state education agency or state university[1]

Generally, such institutions will offer courses applicable toward an associate, bachelor's, advanced, or professional degree; hold scheduled meetings between instructor and student; and utilize a physical plant of some sort for these classes. This omits exclusively correspondence schools; vocational schools (if they do not also have an academic curriculum); business colleges and other institutions offering training for specific commercial fields; the schools of the armed forces (but not the service academies and some in-service institutions such as the Air Force Institute of Technology); formal classroom training provided for employees by private business firms; and other efforts not meeting the aforementioned conventions.

In this study the term *higher education* coincides with the definition used by the federal government. This is not to disparage the efforts of other schools serving post–high school students; rather, it is simply because here the major interest will be the very institutions which the federal government defines as "institutions of higher learning." Another important consideration is that comprehensive data do not exist for most post–high school institutions other than those classified by the government as institutions of higher learning (hereafter referred to as IHL).

Within the broad group of IHL, there are two other divisions: (1) the type of institution by level and nature of degree programs offered and (2) whether the institution is public or private. Each of these two divisions will be explained in turn.

1. U.S. Dept. of HEW, Office of Education, *Education Directory, 1968–1969*, Pt. 3 (Washington, D.C.: GPO, 1969), p. 1.

There are six types of IHL described by function or degree-mix: (1) the *university*, an institution with professional schools (law and medicine, for example) as well as a college of arts and sciences, which places heavy emphasis on graduate and advanced study; (2) the *four-year college*, which often offers programs of more than four years in length, but places dominant emphasis on the bachelor's degree programs in both the arts and sciences; (3) the *seminary* or *theological school*, also a four-year school; (4) the *technological* or *special professional school* which offers degree programs in a limited number of fields and a small number of courses in some liberal disciplines; (5) the *academic junior college* which places emphasis on courses directly transferable to four-year colleges and universities; and (6) the *vocational junior college* which offers few academic courses. The primary distinctions, however, are (1) the university, (2) the four-year college, and (3) the junior college. These distinctions will be the only ones used hereafter.

The various IHL are also denoted *public* or *private*, a distinction which, in most cases, turns on whether or not the subject institution receives a regular credit to its operating budget from a state or local government unit. This distinction does not, however, cover all cases, and officially the private institution is to be distinguished from the public school in that the former is governed by a body not representing any particular governmental subdivision. It will be seen later that the substantive differences between public and private institutions are due to matters other than the official nature of the governing board.

Thus, with higher education defined, and individual institutions distinguished as to functional type and governance, the macro- and microeconomic characteristics of American higher education may be examined. The purposes of this analysis will be to acquire an understanding of the existing nature of higher education and to interpret this in terms of national economic aggregates.

Macroeconomic Characteristics of American Higher Education

Higher education in the United States absorbs the energies of more persons in the working-age groups than any other industry. A conservative estimate for 1967 indicates that higher education absorbed in terms of full-time equivalent (FTE) persons 5.5 million students, 550 thousand professional persons, and about 570 thousand other employees, for a total of about 6.6 million FTE persons. This contrasts with about 3.8 million persons employed in primary and secondary schooling and 2.4 million providing medical services. The labor intensity of education per se may be seen when it is considered that the aggregate of all persons engaged in the provision of formal education, at all levels, in 1968 was about triple the number of employees in the electrical machinery industry, the leading employer of all the durable goods industries. And, when the FTEs of all persons sixteen or older engaged in either receiving or providing formal education are summed, this sum exceeds total employment in all durable goods industries.[2]

The only detailed statistics available on actual employment in higher education pertain to professional personnel. (Data available on nonprofessional personnel in IHL are not detailed as to type of task(s) performed, nor have they been collected long enough to trace secular trends.) Table 1.1 presents some data on professional employees in IHL for recent years.

During this same period from 1955 to 1963, the total civilian labor force increased about 10.5 percent.[3] From Table 1.1

2. U.S. Dept. of HEW, Office of Education, *Numbers and Characteristics of Employees in Institutions of Higher Education, Fall 1966* (Washington, D.C.: GPO, 1969) and U.S. Dept. of Commerce, Office of Business Economics, *Survey of Current Business*, July 1969 (Washington, D.C.: GPO).

3. The National Industrial Conference Board, *Economic Almanac, 1967–1968* (New York: Macmillan, 1967).

TABLE 1.1

TOTAL EMPLOYMENT OF PROFESSIONAL PERSONS, ALL HIGHER EDUCATION,
SELECTED YEARS, FALL, 1955–63

Classification	1963	1961	1959	1957	1955
All professional persons	498,359	427,833	382,664	348,509	301,582
Public IHL	288,165	235,851	209,643	189,834	161,345
Private IHL	210,194	191,982	173,021	158,675	140,237
FTE teachers[a]	237,367	208,277	189,256	177,000	—
Public IHL	131,241	111,799	101,113	95,423	—
Private IHL	106,126	96,478	88,170	82,131	—
Organized research	65,088	50,058	37,099	32,531	27,056
Public IHL	38,005	27,857	22,368	19,669	16,648
Private IHL	27,083	22,201	14,731	12,862	10,408
General administration and student services	46,247	37,408	34,362	28,898	22,223
Public IHL	20,478	15,517	13,636	11,382	8,687
Private IHL	25,769	21,881	20,726	17,516	13,536
Library	12,539	11,025	9,939	9,099	8,515
Public IHL	6,464	5,592	4,957	4,524	4,126
Private IHL	6,075	5,433	4,982	4,575	4,389

SOURCE: U.S. Dept. of HEW, Office of Education, *Faculty and Other Professional Staff in Institutions of Higher Learning, First Term 1961–62, Fall Term 1963–64* (Washington, D.C.: GPO).

[a] With rank of instructor and above.

the following percentage increases in professional personnel in IHL, over this same period, may be computed:

All Professional Persons	65.2%
FTE Teachers	104.3%
Organized Research	140.2%
General Administration and Student Services	108.1%
Library	47.2%

The subcategories in Table 1.1 do not total all professional personnel, thus it is obvious that some omitted groups are not growing as fast as instructors, administrators, and researchers. (Extension is a good example of a slowly growing category.) However, it suffices to note that higher education is a growth industry, and, in terms of total professional IHL personnel versus the total civilian labor force, grew about six times as fast as the economy as a whole between 1955 and 1963. And some activities, such as organized research and instruction, grew from ten to thirteen times as fast as the total labor force. This growth may be contrasted with employment trends in the two fastest growing private industries: (1) miscellaneous business services and (2) air transportation. Employment in the former increased 83.3 percent, and in the latter 56.1 percent, between 1955 and 1963.[4]

Rapid employment growth in higher education during the post–Korean War period is largely due to a dramatic growth in enrollments, a broadening in the array of services provided to students, and a boom in sponsored research. The employment growth in organized or sponsored research has already been noted, and much of this can be traced to an increasing tendency for the federal government to subsidize research at the universities.

Between 1961 and 1963, total expenditures by all IHL for organized research increased about $400 million; during the same period, federal funds to universities for research and development increased about $240 million. From 1955 to 1965, federal funds, as a share of the total support for research and development in universities, increased from 40 to 60 percent.[5] The reasons for this significant absolute and relative growth in federal government support of research are many, but it may be noted the Department of Defense and the National Aeronautics and Space

4. U.S. Dept. of Commerce, Office of Business Economics, *The National Income and Product Accounts of the United States, 1929–1965* (Washington, D.C.: GPO, 1967).

5. U.S. Dept. of HEW, Office of Education, *Digest of Educational Statistics, 1968* (Washington, D.C.: GPO) and U.S. Dept. of Commerce, Bureau of the Census, *Statistical Abstract of the United States, 1968* (Washington, D.C.: GPO).

TABLE 1.2

TOTAL DEGREE-CREDIT ENROLLMENTS, ALL HIGHER EDUCATION, SELECTED
YEARS, FALL, 1955–67

Year	All IHL	Public IHL	Private IHL
1967	6,348,000 est.	4,305,000 est.	2,043,000 est.
1965	5,526,325	3,624,442	1,901,883
1963	4,494,626	2,848,454	1,646,172
1961	3,860,643	2,328,912	1,531,731
1959	3,364,861	1,972,457	1,392,404
1957	3,036,938	1,752,669	1,248,269
1955	2,653,034	1,476,282	1,176,752

SOURCE: U.S. Dept. of HEW, Office of Education, *Projections of Educational Statistics to 1977–78* (Washington, D.C.: GPO, 1968).

Administration in 1965 accounted for 82 per cent of the federal research and development obligations.[6]

The most important single factor in the increased total activity of American IHL has been the increase in students. Table 1.2 shows the growth in college students during the post–Korean War period.

The causes of rapid increase in college enrollments are of much interest. First, it may be noted that college enrollments increased about 140 percent between 1955 and 1967, while the national population increased by only one-fifth.[7] One obvious explanation for this wide disparity is that the college-age population has grown much faster in recent years than the total population, a consequence of the baby boom during the 1940s. However, even this will not explain all the divergence between the rate of increase in college enrollments and the total population—one must search for other influences.

Each year it becomes more likely that any given college-age

6. National Science Foundation, *Geographic Distribution of Federal Funds for Research and Development: Fiscal Year 1965* (Washington, D.C.: GPO, 1967), p. 27.

7. Bureau of the Census, *Statistical Abstract, 1968.*

person will be in college. This seems to be the result of a combination of two factors: (1) more students become potential college entrants, given any absolute number of seventeen- to nineteen-year-olds, because an increasing percentage of high school students take high school diplomas and (2) an increasing percentage of these high school graduates enter college. A few statistics will support both observations.

In 1940, when 455 of every 1,000 children who had entered fifth grade in 1932 graduated from high school, the ratio that fall of entering college students to high school graduates the preceding spring was 0.35. In 1967, 721 of every 1,000 students who were fifth graders in 1959 graduated from high school, and the ratio of first time college students to spring high school graduates was 0.56.[8] Thus, not only has college attendance grown spectacularly in recent years because of an abnormal percentage of the population falling in the college-age group, but it is becoming more likely that any given young person will be both qualified and inclined to enter college.

There are some common influences at work on both the high school–completion and college-ongoing rates. First, the education and training needed to acquire promising jobs has surely increased over time and influenced students to lengthen their stays in school. Second, rising real income in most sectors of the economy has made it less necessary for children to begin work at a minor age to supplement the family income. Third, the continuing rural-to-urban shift in population has contributed to this trend because, historically, urban children remain in school longer than their rural peers.[9] Finally, children have been strongly influenced

8. Office of Education, *Educational Statistics*, 1966.

9. Although the mean educational attainment in urban areas is still in excess of that in rural areas, the difference is narrowing. In 1967 the mean years of schooling completed by all residents fourteen or older in standard metropolitan statistical areas was 12.0 years, while the same statistic for the rest of the nation was 11.0 years. See U.S. Dept. of Commerce, Bureau of the Census, *Current Population Reports*, Series P-20, number 169 (Washington, D.C.: GPO, 1968).

by the government to complete high school (for example, by child labor and compulsory attendance laws), and this has worked indirectly on the college-ongoing rate, as would anything that caused a higher percentage of children to complete high school.

However, there are also more subtle influences on the college-ongoing rate that are separate from any change in the high school–completion rate. Robert P. Wolff believes the primary reason for the boom in college-ongoing rates "is simply that for millions of American boys and girls, higher education is the gateway to the middle classes, and a diploma from the best schools is a passport to the upper middle classes. . . . In short, the race for college is a crucial lap in the great race for wealth, position, and power in American society."[10]

Other significant influences on the college-ongoing rate in recent years have been (1) the greater availability of college to many people because of the post–World War II influx of veterans crumbling any remaining class barriers to college attendance and (2) the growth in public junior colleges (to be discussed in more detail below) which serve persons who are not prepared to enter four-year colleges or universities fresh from high school.

One other item of interest in connection with both Tables 1.1 and 1.2 is the relationship between the increases in students and professional staff in IHL. Degree-credit students increased about 70 percent between 1955 and 1963, while instructors grew 104 percent, and personnel in general administration and student services climbed 108 percent. This means a declining ratio of students to personnel, but a good deal of this decline may be due to expanded services and educational programs, a phenomenon noted by others.[11]

   10. Robert P. Wolff, "The Race for College," in *The Troubled Campus*, eds. of *Atlantic* Magazine (Boston: Little, Brown, 1966), p. 134.
   11. Seymour E. Harris, "Financing of Higher Education: Broad Issues," in *Financing Higher Education*, ed. Keezer, p. 43.

TABLE 1.3

TOTAL EXPENDITURES, ALL HIGHER EDUCATION, SELECTED YEARS, 1940–64, IN MILLIONS OF DOLLARS

Year	Education and General	Auxiliary Enterprises and Activities	Gross Real Capital
1964	$7,425	$1,452	$2,208
1962	5,768	1,158	1,550
1960	4,513	916	1,192
1950	1,706	476	417
1940	522	124	84

SOURCE: U.S. Dept. of Commerce, Bureau of the Census, *Statistical Abstract of the United States, 1968* (Washington, D.C.: GPO).

The most pertinent macroeconomic statistics for higher education are those concerning finances. Table 1.3 lists actual operating and capital expenditures of all IHL for selected years in the post–Great Depression period.

Between 1940 and 1964, total expenditures for higher education increased 1,235 percent, while current gross national product rose 534 percent; in the 1960–64 period, higher education spending climbed 67 percent while GNP increased but one-fourth. These statistics buttress earlier arguments and show that higher education has been a growth industry in the recent past.

Finally, the indirect costs of higher education must be considered. The overwhelming portion of the total indirect costs of higher education is the opportunity costs of having, for example, 6.3 million working-age persons in college, rather than in the labor force, in 1967–68. Schultz and Becker have calculated wages forgone by students individually, but not for the economy as a whole. Schultz comments:

> What would the earnings of school-age workers have been if all of them had entered the labor market? But the question is not

relevant because our problem is not one that entails a large shift in the number of human agents. . . . Instead, we want to know *what earnings a typical student has been foregoing at the margin.*[12] [Emphasis added.]

Obviously, there is a significant conceptual and statistical difference between the effect on the whole economy of one student attending college and not producing goods and services for nine months, as opposed to 6.3 million students doing one or the other. A hypothetical thrusting of all college students out of their institutions, an exercise necessary to estimate aggregate income forgone, would have to consider that

1. The increased supply of workers would make observable compensation rates meaningless.
2. Since about 40 percent of all college students are female, it would be unreasonable to assume all collegians are potential additions to the labor force as commonly defined.[13]
3. Unemployment rates in the relevant age groups would be affected drastically by a mass exodus from IHL.

Thus, although it is certain the nation sacrifices some short-run output by keeping large numbers of working-age people in college, the long-run effect is less certain. In fact, it seems safe only to say that the net long-run contribution to total long-run output, by virtue of this public willingness to keep the large numbers in college, is probably a positive one. But estimation of the magnitude of this positive effect is well beyond the scope

12. Theordore W. Schultz, "Capital Formation by Education," *Journal of Political Economy* 68, no. 6 (December 1960): 74–75.

13. In January 1967 there were, in the United States, about 9,089,000 college-age females. Of this total 1,641,000 were in school; 3,656,000 were neither in school nor in the labor force; and the remaining 5,533,000 were either working or seeking work. This is a participation rate of 41 percent for the nonschool, eighteen-to twenty-four-year-old females. The unemployment rate was about 9 percent. See National Industrial Conference Board, *Economic Almanac, 1967–1968*.

of the present study, and we wish only to note in passing the phenomenon of indirect costs.

Microeconomic Characteristics of American Higher Education

This section discusses four microeconomic aspects of American IHL: (1) the numbers and types of IHL, (2) the distribution of these IHL in terms of enrollments, (3) some rather unusual characteristics of the higher education "firm," and (4) a few average measures which are basically manipulations of aggregates already presented in Tables 1.1 through 1.3. The analyses of this section will be of use later when specific institutional data are examined in more detail. Table 1.4 traces the recent trend in both numbers and types of IHL.

TABLE 1.4

TOTAL INSTITUTIONS, SELECTED YEARS, 1961–67

Year	TWO-YEAR IHL			ALL OTHER IHL			TOTAL IHL
	Public	Private	Both	Public	Private	Both	
1967	520	266	786	414	1,174	1,588	2,374
1965	420	259	679	401	1,150	1,551	2,230
1963	381	263	644	381	1,114	1,495	2,139
1961	346	247	593	375	1,072	1,447	2,040

SOURCE: U.S. Dept. of HEW, Office of Education, *Digest of Educational Statistics*, 1962, 1964, 1966, and 1968 (Washington, D.C.: GPO).

Since it seems reasonable to assume there would be some kind of time lag measured in at least months—and likely years—before a school could go from the proposal to the operating state, the data in Table 1.4 can be taken to reflect the extent to which phenomena in the late 1950s and early 1960s influenced the change in the numbers of IHL. Between 1961 and 1967, the net

increase in IHL was 334, or 16.4 percent. About three-fifths
of this increase came in two-year schools. All public institutions
increased about three times as fast as all private schools. The
most dynamic group of institutions was the public two-year
schools, increasing 53 percent; at the other extreme, private
two-year schools increased less than 8 percent. In 1961 private
IHL outnumbered public IHL 65 to 35; by 1967 this ratio was
55 to 45.

Many factors are behind this differential growth of IHL. But
at this point, it may be observed that the public sector has been
vigorous in providing an increased higher educational opportunity, and this is especially manifested in the growth of community colleges. On the other hand, the private institutions have
been subject to financial influences which have made their
existence a little trying.

There is significant disparity in the size of public and private
institutions. Tables 1.5 and 1.6 and Figures 1.1 through 1.3
show this disparity.

TABLE 1.5
SIZE DISTRIBUTION, ALL PUBLIC INSTITUTIONS, 1967

Students	UNIVERSITY		4-YEAR		2-YEAR	
	IHL	Total Students	IHL	Total Students	IHL	Total Students
Under 200	—	—	1	192	20	2,076
200–499	—	—	12	4,532	67	23,889
500–999	—	—	29	22,182	119	87,594
1,000–2,499	—	—	79	137,507	151	231,587
2,500–4,999	2	8,637	87	320,669	95	339,899
5,000–9,999	20	150,089	89	653,912	38	257,417
10,000–19,999	36	541,703	16	212,884	27	349,828
20,000 and over	34	1,172,848	9	218,821	3	79,763
Total	92	1,873,277	322	1,570,698	520	1,372,053

SOURCE: Office of Education, *Educational Statistics, 1968.*

TABLE 1.6

Size Distribution, All Private Institutions, 1967

Students	University		4-Year		2-Year	
	IHL	Total Students	IHL	Total Students	IHL	Total Students
Under 200	—	—	185	20,445	85	8,849
200–499	—	—	175	61,177	91	30,886
500–999	—	—	325	237,897	58	39,999
1,000–2,499	1	1,751	333	490,941	26	38,294
2,500–4,999	9	34,379	70	224,560	6	22,681
5,000–9,999	29	217,486	17	113,259	—	—
10,000–19,999	17	233,972	4	51,486	—	—
20,000 and over	8	228,144	1	39,514	—	—
Total	64	715,732	1,110	1,239,279	266	140,709

Source: Office of Education, *Educational Statistics, 1968.*

Several things emerge from these illustrations. Most striking is the tendency for public institutions to be much larger than private institutions of similar function; although 70 percent of all American college students were attending public institutions in 1967, there were more private than public IHL. Also, not only do private institutions tend to be smaller than their public counterparts, they tend to be *drastically* smaller; only 6.5 percent of all private universities and four-year colleges in 1967 had 5,000 or more students, while one out of two similar public IHL had at least 5,000 students. Finally, each of the three types of public IHL, in the aggregate, enrolled about equal total numbers of students; in contrast, the private four-year colleges had better than 61 percent of *all* students attending private institutions. This drastic difference in the size distribution of public versus private IHL will play a crucial role in the implications of economies of scale for the financial health of any IHL!

One characteristic of American IHL, which Gordon N. Ray discusses, pervades their microeconomic nature:

FIGURE 1.1

PERCENTAGE DISTRIBUTION, PUBLIC AND PRIVATE UNIVERSITIES, ALL
RESIDENT STUDENTS, FALL, 1967

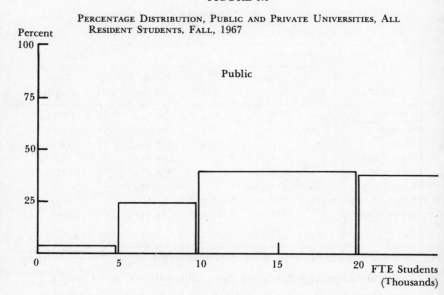

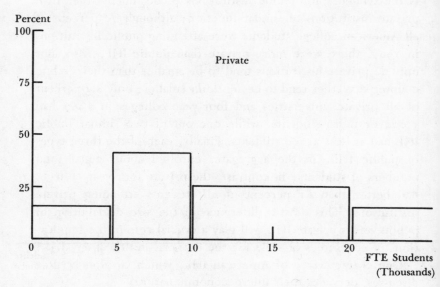

FIGURE 1.2
PERCENTAGE DISTRIBUTION, PUBLIC AND PRIVATE FOUR-YEAR
COLLEGES, ALL RESIDENT STUDENTS, FALL, 1967

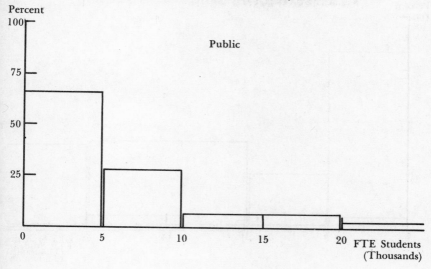

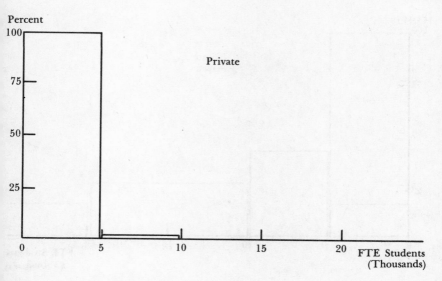

FIGURE 1.3

PERCENTAGE DISTRIBUTION, PUBLIC AND PRIVATE JUNIOR COLLEGES, ALL RESIDENT STUDENTS, FALL, 1967

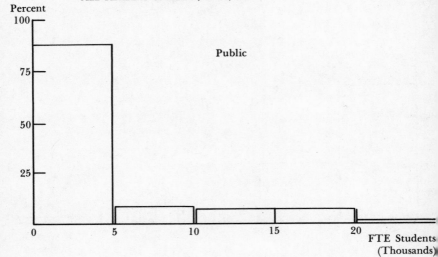

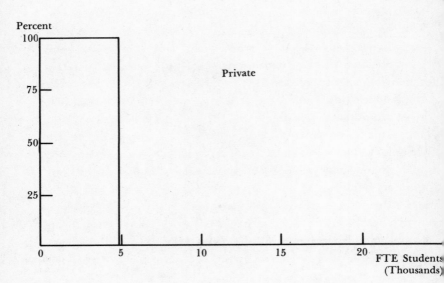

A college or university is not a corporation or a government department. Members of its faculty are not employees or civil servants. Academic administrators are not "management" or superior bureaucrats. Instead, faculty and administrators alike belong to a community of scholars with which the decision in all matters of educational policy should rest.[14]

Notwithstanding the unique relationship among all professional personnel in most American IHL, resources are still necessary to conduct operations. In the tradition of American higher education, many groups supply the necessary funds for operations, and some share, with the academic community, the responsibility for establishing institutional objectives and policies. We may identify some of these groups.

Public institutions depend upon the various governments for some portion of the funds they finally spend. In turn, governments usually have a formal voice in the school's level of activity because they are able to vary the amount of revenue made available. At one extreme there will be four governmental agencies exercising such influence; for some community colleges, there are but two.

A measure of the governmental entities to which a public school is subject would be the number to which the institution must appeal for funds. The majority of the states today have what are called *coordinating boards* for the public IHL in the state, and a major purpose of these boards is to review the several schools' requests for funds from state sources. Also, the *governor* will review and make recommendations on the institutions' requests because, in most states, the public IHL are part of the executive branch. A third governmental agency is the *legislature*, which hears from the schools because it makes the appropriations to the schools' accounts. Finally, the *governing board*, which is a governmental agency, normally serves as the original reviewer

14. Ray, "Conflict and Cooperation," p. 105.

of budget proposals from the academic community. Therefore, four state governmental agencies (coordinating board, governor, legislature, and governing board) exist to say yes or no to some part of the institutions' request for funds *which are, in the last analysis, statements of proposed institutional policy!* At the other extreme, a community college, which is part of a public school district with power to tax, is affected only de jure by (1) the school board setting the property tax levy and (2) the property assessor determining the value of the tax base. However, in practice the assessor is not recognized as having much direct influence on the total appropriation to the school. Of course, if the state provides financial aid to community colleges, the state legislature and governor will also be decision-making entities.

For private IHL the situation is more diverse because of various relations between institutions and private benefactors, actual and potential. For all but the most powerful and respected institutions, major donors may well play a role in the finances, and thus the activities of the school, similar to that played by the state governments vis-à-vis public IHL. Certainly, in most instances it is not strictly true that "the decisions in all matters of academic policy" are made by a "community of scholars."

Although the four- and two-year colleges devote almost all of their efforts to undergraduate instruction of resident students, the university is something else. Cartter gives the following characterization of the contemporary university: "Turning to the individual institution, the closest analogy one can draw between a university and a business firm is to picture the former as a firm producing multiple products." [15] A well-known economist, Carl Kaysen, gives a more technical explanation:

> The . . . universities typically produce at least four sets of outputs of rather different sorts: liberal education, preprofessional and

15. Cartter, "Economics of the University," p. 483.

professional education, applied research . . . , and fundamental research and the preservation of knowledge and, more broadly, culture. These outputs have complex interrelations in both production and use: typically, production of one involves production of another as well, and frequently the consumers desire some mixture of the separate products.[16]

Higher education is also somewhat unusual in that it billets some of its own consumers and provides them with an increasing array of goods and services. In being all things to all men, the modern university is a conglomerate, producing multiple products, in one of the nation's prime growth industries.

American IHL are labor-intensive enterprises in which there has been really little technological change in centuries. One observer, Harold F. Clark, writes the following:

> [Printing and general distribution of books] was one of the great technological changes that occurred in education. . . . It would certainly be reasonable to assume . . . more could be learned in a given period of years if pupils had books to read, as compared to schools without books. . . .
>
> There is no reason why machines that can talk should not make a further increase in teacher efficiency. These technological devices include television, motion pictures, radio, filmstrips, tape recorders, teaching machines, and many other devices. Unfortunately, there is no school in the world that has seriously tried to determine the extent to which these technological devices can further increase the efficiency of the teacher.[17]

Why do changes lag in an industry so responsible for the technological change in other parts of the economy? Certainly, one important reason is that education involves more than just conveying information, and we today are not even clear on what

16. Carl Kaysen, "Some General Observations on the Pricing of Higher Education," in *Higher Education in the United States*, ed. Harris, p. 56.

17. Harold F. Clark, *Cost and Quality in Public Education* (Syracuse, N.Y.: Syracuse University Press, 1963), p. 27.

influences the educational experience, and in what ways. As Philip H. Coombs points out, "Educators are often tempted to judge [educational quality] by such measures as expenditures per student, the student-teacher ratio, and the number of books in the library. But that is like judging an automobile or a suit of clothes . . . by the factory conditions under which it was produced." [18] In short, it is difficult to have much innovation in the combination of inputs if the output cannot be evaluated. The second reason is that the decision-making apparatus in IHL is conservative and cumbersome. Willard L. Thorp writes:

> There is a prejudice against change in many educational enterprises, as there is in all established institutions. This is augmented by the dispersion of responsibility among faculty, administration, and trustees. . . . The faculty is responsible for the curriculum but not for the budget; the trustees must be responsible for solvency but cannot interfere with the structure of costs; and the administration has few prerogatives in either of these fields except to act as stimulant and lubricant. [19]

But perhaps, in the last analysis, the intransigence of IHL to changing technology can be traced to "the widely held view that the concept of efficiency does not apply to education . . . many persons are under the misapprehension that the effort to increase efficiency necessarily and ordinarily changes the goals of education." [20] Whatever the reasons, the interesting result is that by no means should higher education be considered a technologically dynamic industry.

A rather novel characteristic of higher education is that the industry simultaneously "produces" manpower for its own needs, as well as for the needs of other industries. Aside from the novelty of this situation, an interesting question involves the

18. Coombs, "An Economist's Overview," p. 16.

19. Willard L. Thorp, "Probabilities and Possibilities," in *Financing Higher Education*, ed. Keezer, p. 291.

20. Clark, *Cost and Quality*, p. 11.

priorities decision makers, within IHL, place on these somewhat competing demands for graduates. At least a portion of the nonacademic world seems to have no doubts about the ordering of these priorities. They are certain that IHL place a superior priority on preparing students for positions within the academic community, and this unsettling opinion is manifested in statements to the effect that educational programs are "too academic" or "fail to meet the needs of business."

Of course, it can be argued that any graduate who is prepared to take an academic position is also acceptable to most nonacademic employers; in effect, the line of reasoning is that requirements for employment in the academic community are not mutually exclusive from the requirements of the nonacademic world. In any event the purpose here in raising the issue is only to center on a rather unusual microeconomic characteristic of higher education, not to settle related issues.

A most perplexing element of the microeconomics of higher education, especially for laymen, is the practice of IHL charging individual recipients of their products less than full average costs for producing these products. And, in fact, the common practice is to charge individual recipients less than full average variable costs. This practice, of course, requires augmentation of the institutional operating and capital budgets from other sources, thus giving rise to the multiparty decision making discussed above. However, most members of the academic community (and many outside this group as well) support such pricing practices, most often on the basis of the following reasons:

1. There are both individual and collective benefits realized from the products of IHL; the collective benefits accrue to society at large, thus society should contribute resources towards the provision of the products.

2. The individual benefits of higher education should not be restricted only to those able to afford the full average costs of providing higher education.
3. Institutions will debase the quality of their products if forced to rely solely on contributions from individual recipients because (presumably) these recipients value above all else the *evidence* of having received the product.

Each of these arguments will be discussed in turn.

It is commonly argued that higher education "is a 'general public service' which, through its implied consequences affects . . . society as a whole [and] it is, therefore, proper that all citizens should contribute towards the provision of this public service."[21] Such positions have elicited the following comment from Seymour Harris: "Administrators of public institutions emphasize especially the relation of pricing [of higher education] to the national gain . . . and hence the inference is that tuition should be low because society primarily gains. Here, indeed, is an argument for tuition below costs. But fortunately the student gains, and increasingly so as higher education becomes more and more vocational."[22]

Another observation can be made concerning the practice of pricing IHL's products at below costs to individual recipients: Mere presence of spill-over benefits from provision of a rather individual product has not, in this country, resulted automatically in collective fiscal support. For example, the highway and street system benefits even those who do not own or operate motor vehicles. These indirect benefits come in the form of more products available at lower costs, more efficient police work, firefighting, and emergency medical services; and a low-cost, alternative mode of intercity commercial transportation. How-

21. Papi, "General Problems of the Economics of Education," p. 8.
22. Harris, "Broad Issues," p. 58.

ever, charges to direct consumers of highways and streets have dominated highway finance in this country, both philosophically and in practice.

On the other hand, higher education does not stand alone as something yielding collective and private benefits simultaneously, and receiving some public subsidy (ostensibly) for this reason. Local public health operations fall into the same category. The point is that, rightly or wrongly, collective support for the provision of products that also carry significant private benefits has been mostly a matter of chance, history, and custom in this country. Higher education just happens to be one of the areas receiving collective support, and will continue to receive it in the future simply because the custom is firmly established.

Few today will argue that higher education should be available only to those who are able to pay the substantial average costs of its provision. It may be argued, however, that uniformly low tuition is an inferior way to meet what is, basically, a problem of personal income distribution. In addition, it may well be that money is *not* the major factor inhibiting poor youths from attending college. Indeed, if college is an upper-middle-class institution, it is not surprising that attendance by lower-class youth has been subject to many subtle influences. The point is that subsidized tuition may *not* make much of a contribution towards democratizing the society, and could well result in nothing more than a subsidy to a class of society which little needs it.

If direct receivers of the products of higher education are concerned only with the evidence of such receipt (and little concerned about the substance), and if one accepts the proposition that, in this case, the customer is *not* always right, below-cost pricing of IHL's products probably makes sense. However, it is difficult to imagine procurers, in the main, of applied research and preprofessional or professional education, holding this attitude. The argument stands or falls on the validity of assumptions which may be more appropriate for younger students than those who attend college.

Another peculiarity of the pricing of IHL's products is the common practice of commodity price discrimination (in an economic, although not legal, sense), especially when more than just liberal education is dispensed. Many universities charge students identical fees whether enrolled in, say, the graduate program in economics or the undergraduate program in the college of arts and sciences. This is common in spite of evidence, even with rudimentary cost accounting, that per-student costs of the former have been shown once to be about tenfold those of the latter. [23] And perhaps just as common, the differences in charges for various programs (when such differential charges do exist) usually do not seem to reflect accurately cost differences. We wish to observe this phenomenon rather than explain it because such explanation would be lengthier than could be here justified, given that the object of this study is cost analysis, not the interaction of demand and cost.

Finally, we turn to a combination of data, previously presented, to obtain some "average" statistics on IHL. It should be cautioned at the outset that, primarily because of the great diversity among IHL, average data mean less than would be the case in many other industries. Nevertheless, it may be helpful to reduce some of the aggregate statistical data presented above to an institutional and student basis.

Table 1.7 presents some of the more salient average statistics on American IHL for 1957–58, 1963–64, and the percentage change for each statistic.

During this six-year period, the implicit price deflator for gross national product, state and local government purchases

---

23. *California and Western Conference Cost and Statistical Study* (Berkeley: University of California, n.d.).

TABLE 1.7

SUMMARY MICROECONOMIC STATISTICS, ALL IHL, 1957–58 and 1963–64, PERCENT CHANGE

Item	1963–64	1957–58	Percent Change
Current educational expenditure, per institution[a]			
Public IHL	$3,536,000	$2,303,000	53.5
Private IHL	1,465,000	927,000	58.0
Current educational expenditure, per degree-credit student[b]			
Public IHL	955	868	10.0
Private IHL	1,218	913	33.4
Ratio of degree-credit students to FTE faculty members with rank of instructor and above			
Public IHL	21.7	18.4	17.9
Private IHL	15.5	15.6	(0.6)
Ratio of all degree-credit students to administrative personnel[c]			
Public IHL	139.1	154.0	(9.7)
Private IHL	63.9	73.3	(12.8)
Ratio of all FTE degree-credit students to all FTE instructional staff			
All IHL[d]	15.4	13.4	15.0

SOURCES: U.S. Dept. of HEW, Office of Education, *Biennial Survey of Education in the United States, 1956–58* (Washington, D.C.: GPO, 1960) and *Educational Statistics,* 1962 and 1966.

[a] *Educational expenditure* is here taken to mean total current educational and general expenditures minus expenditures for organized research, extension, public service, and other activities.

[b] Educational expenditures are for a twelve-month period, while degree-credit students is for the fall term only. A lesser percentage of private than public schools conduct summer sessions, and caution should be exercised when interpreting the data of the two types of schools.

[c] *Administrative personnel* is here synonymous with "General administration and student services" personnel as used in Table 1.1.

[d] Estimates of FTE degree-credit students are available for all schools, but not for public and private schools separately.

of goods and services, rose about 21 percent.[24] Applied to current educational expenditure, per degree-credit student, in Table 1.7, this imperfect measure of price movements during 1957–64 for all IHL would, nonetheless, indicate that real expenditures per student at public IHL declined 8 percent, while at private schools they rose about 10 percent. The remainder of Table 1.7 would tentatively suggest that public institutions in effect traded, in real terms, teachers for administrative and service personnel, with the decline of the former exceeding the increase in the latter, the result being some decrease in real costs per student. On the other hand, the same analysis would suggest that private IHL did not experience increases in the student-teacher ratio but did allow the ratio of administrative and service personnel to students to increase about 13 percent, and the outcome contributed to the aforementioned 10 percent rise in real expenditures per student. Again, this analysis is tentative and far from rigorous; but the evidence seems to suggest that something of this kind did occur.

The one other item of interest in Table 1.7 is current educational expenditures, per institution. The wide disparity between public and private IHL is, of course, a reflection of wide differences in the scale of the two types of institutions, a fact noted above (see pp. 24–25).

As a last analysis, a look at the revenue and expenditure patterns of IHL is in order. Table 1.8 presents a percentage distribution of both current revenues and expenditures, for both public and private IHL, during the two most recent years for which data were available, as well as for 1957–58, to examine change over time.

There are several observations of interest to be derived from Table 1.8. First, in both public and private IHL, the contributions by the federal government to revenues and the expenditures by

24. Office of Business Economics, *National Income Accounts*.

TABLE 1.8

TOTAL CURRENT REVENUES AND EXPENDITURES: PERCENTAGE ANALYSIS, ALL IHL,
1957–58, 1961–62, and 1963–64

Item	PUBLIC IHL			PRIVATE IHL		
	1963–64	1961–62	1957–58	1963–64	1961–62	1957–58
Revenue						
Student charges	10.9	10.4	10.3	31.2	32.4	32.9
State and local governments	43.0	45.0	42.5	1.5	1.7	1.4
Federal government	19.6	18.6	14.8	26.5	23.2	15.9
Other	24.5	26.0	32.4	40.8	42.7	49.7
	100.0	100.0	100.0	100.0	100.0	100.0
Expenditures						
Instruction and departmental research	33.5	33.2	34.3	26.9	27.9	30.3
General administration and general expense	8.9	8.4	8.5	12.4	12.5	13.1
Organized research	18.3	18.5	15.3	25.5	23.2	17.2
Other	39.3	39.9	41.9	35.2	36.4	39.4
	100.0	100.0	100.0	100.0	100.0	100.0

SOURCES: Office of Education, *Biennial Survey of Education* and *Educational Statistics*, 1962 and 1966.

the institutions on organized research, present a remarkable correlation. This is not to imply that all organized research is financed directly by the federal government—but the relation between the two is much more than casual. Second, on the revenue side, there has been great constancy in the shares contributed by students to both public and private IHL, and by state and local government to the public schools. (The contribution by state and local governments to private IHL has also been a stable percentage, but this is a minor source of revenue for these schools.) Third, on the expenditure side, the three most labor-intensive functions (instruction, administration, and research) are absorbing an increasing share of the total budget. Put another way, "other" expenditures (library, plant operation and maintenance, auxiliary enterprises, and student aid) are decreasing in relative importance for both types of IHL, although this change is a little more dynamic in the public schools. Last, there are rather significant differences, in public as opposed to private IHL, in the share of total expenditures going to instruction & departmental research and general administration & general expense. These latter two observations will play a significant role in the theory of returns to scale in higher education to be developed in the remainder of this study.

Summary

The term *higher education*, as used in this study, coincides with the definition of such institutions used by the federal government. Basically, the concept includes institutions conducting classes in a physical plant of some sort, for resident students, with the courses applicable to an associate, bachelor's, or advanced degree. Designated institutions of higher learning are further denoted as universities, four-year schools, and two-year institutions by the level of the most advanced degree offered and the relative emphasis on graduate and professional study. A final distinction is between public and private IHL, and it is officially determined by whether or not the institution's governing board is an agency of some governmental subdivision; if a board is a governmental entity, the institution is said to be public. (This is to make a distinction from a private college which may be incorporated by the state.)

There are two outstanding characteristics of American higher education when compared to the economy as a whole: (1) higher education, by far, absorbs more working-age persons than any other industry and (2) the industry is experiencing growth greatly out of proportion to the remainder of the economy. The second characteristic has given rise to the first, and it may be noted that the major influences on higher education's growth rate are (1) the federal government's stimulus to organized research activity, (2) an expansion of the supporting services extended to the student, and (3) a rapid increase in students in the post–Korean War period. This latter phenomenon has been affected by the baby boom of 1940–50, but a more important influence has been a dramatic increase in the high school–completion and college-ongoing rates. An important, but largely unquantified, macroeconomic aspect of higher education is the short-run opportunity cost of having large numbers of working-age persons in college and not producing goods and services.

Higher education has many distinguishing microeconomic characteristics. The different types of IHL have grown at different rates in recent years, with the public junior college growing faster than any other type of school, and all public institutions increasing faster than their private equivalents. Public IHL tend to be much larger than private schools. Both public and private institutions usually exist with a unique relationship between administrator and nonadministrator, called the academic community, but in practice those from outside this community, supplying funds to the institutions, acquire a more or less effective voice in the establishment of institutional policy. The IHL are not technologically dynamic. The industry trains its own future personnel, with little recourse to other sources, but these same trained persons have many job alternatives. The IHL charge direct recipients of its products less than full variable costs, often are producers of multiple products, and typically engage in commodity price discrimination.

From 1957 to 1964, real per-student expenditures in the "average" public IHL fell about 8 per cent, but rose about 10 percent in the private schools. It appears that part of the reason for this was a trade of teaching personnel per student for less than commensurate increases in per-student administrative and other professional personnel at public IHL; on the other hand, the student-teacher ratio in private schools rose not at all, while support professionals per student were increasing.

Finally, analysis of the budget composition lends more support to the notion that research activity and federal government support of IHL are closely related. In the near past, students have contributed a rather stable share of revenue to both public and private IHL, and state and local governments have done likewise for public IHL. The professional labor-intensive activities are absorbing an increasing share of the total expenditures at all IHL. However, the latter tendency seems more pronounced at the public institutions, a fact that becomes important in the later analysis of economies of scale in higher education.

With an overview of American higher education completed, it is now time to turn to the primary task of the study, the development and test of a theory of long-run per-student instructional costs in American IHL. In Chapters 2 and 3 an a priori model of expenditures in American IHL is developed. Chapter 4 presents a statistical quantification of this a priori theory. Finally, Chapter 5 contains some observations concerning what seem to be some important implications of this theory.

2

The Theory of Long-Run Costs in Higher Education: Some Preliminary Matters

This is the first of two chapters concerned with developing a theory of the nature of long-run operating costs in American IHL, a theory primarily relating long-run costs to the scale of operations measured in terms of total students, but also considering other exogenous variables which may affect these costs. Although various cost concepts are relevant (for example, total costs, average costs, and marginal costs), it will be convenient to couch the analysis in terms of average costs, especially long-run average costs. Of course, all cost concepts are basically alternative ways of saying roughly the same thing—in Chapter 4, this observation will be developed explicitly.

The chapter considers four matters preliminary to an intensive analysis of the sundry specific activities of IHL. First, a rather elementary overview of the meaning of the microeconomic phenomenon of long-run average costs is presented. It is followed by discussion of the problems inherent in the application of a body of cost theory, really intended for manufacturing and processing operations, to something like a college or university. Next, some broad and pervasive influences on the costs at all IHL are considered. The chapter concludes with a definitional discussion of some key concepts to be used in the remainder of the study.

Long-Run Average Costs for the Firm

Microeconomics is a study of the

> economic activities of such individual economic units as consumers, resource owners, and business firms. It is concerned with the flow of goods and services from business firms to consumers, the composition of the flow, and the evaluation or pricing of the component parts of the flow. It is concerned, too, with the flow of productive resources (or their services) from resource owners to business firms, with their evaluation and with their allocation among alternative uses.[1]

A body of such systematic study would be concerned with markets (both resource and product) and with both demand and supply in these markets, under any conditions of industry structure. Also, the analysis would be unrestricted as to time, studying conditions and phenomena in both the long and short run.

In this study a particular bit of the larger body of microeconomic theory will be utilized. That is, one market (the market for post–secondary school academic training and education) and one group of suppliers in this market (conventionally defined institutions of higher learning) will be examined as to conditions on one side of the market (the supply or cost side) within a special time framework (the long run). In short the study considers the long-run costs incurred by IHL to provide education and training to high school graduates.

Economic theory of the producing entity (or firm), during a period in which the quantities of all factors of production can be varied, is dominated by the principle of *internal* economies of, or returns to, scale. This principle suggests that "a very

1. Richard H. Leftwich, *The Price System and Resource Allocation*, rev. ed. (New York: Holt, Rinehart & Winston), p. 8.

small firm is quite inefficient; as the firm becomes larger, it tends to become more efficient reaching a minimum cost per unit of output at some particular scale.''[2] The firm's attainment of these minimum costs per unit, or maximum internal economies of scale, is usually attributed to ''(1) increasing possibilities of division and specialization of labor and (2) increasing possibilities of using advanced technological developments and/or larger machines''[3] as the scale of output increases. Each of these two explanations for internal economies of scale (hereafter called simply *economies of scale*) deserve further elaboration.

As Adam Smith wrote almost two hundred years ago, a productive process, using labor in single, specialized tasks, will expend less labor per unit, for each task in the complete process, than would be the case if one worker performed all tasks.[4] However, if the scale of a firm's operation is so small that performance of each task necessary for a day's production would require less than a full day's labor, the firm has the choice of (1) specializing in their use of labor (using each worker in his speciality but for only a portion of the day) or (2) using a smaller number of total workers with each engaged all day performing many of the required tasks less efficiently than would specialized workers. The latter choice is more rational for the small-scale firm; in this case specialization of labor is irrational, *although actual labor per unit of output would be less if the labor force were more specialized than if not.* The crux of the matter for the small firm is that specialized labor constitutes a *discontinuous* factor of production. It is employed in lumps (like an eight-hour day), and the scale of output must allow full utilization of this discontinuous resource to make its employment rational. Adam

2. Joe S. Bain, *Price Theory* (New York: Holt, Rinehart & Winston, 1963), p. 112.

3. Leftwich, *The Price System*, p. 156.

4. Adam Smith, *An Inquiry into the Nature and Causes of the Wealth of Nations: Selections*, Book 1 (Chicago: Henry Regnery Co., 1953), chapters 1–3.

Smith's explanation that the division of labor was limited by the size of the market was analogous to saying the division of labor is limited, for the firm, by the scale of output.

The ability to use more efficient technology and machinery, as the scale of output increases, is a special case of the discontinuous factor principle. One may purchase a machine for, say, $1 million with a capacity of 500,000 units per day, and use it to produce the daily output of 100 units. However, if the output level is not expected soon to rise much above 100 units daily, it is more rational to buy a machine that, say, has a daily capacity of 200 units and costs $1,000. The more expensive machine is certainly the more efficient when both operate at capacity; but the small firm cannot make rational use of this high-capacity machine. In effect, the small firm cannot rationally use highly efficient and specialized machinery for the same reason it cannot make rational use of highly efficient and specialized labor: both are *too discontinuous*. Therefore, in the last analysis, economies of scale may be traced to the more efficient use of discontinuous factors of production as a direct result of an increasing level of output.

A word is also in order concerning the behavior of long-run average costs when output climbs past the point that allows maximum economies of scale. Bain writes that after the point of minimum long-run average costs is reached, "further expansion up to some still larger scale may have little effect on unit costs, which remain constant with increases in capacity. But if the scale of the firm is made still larger, it is thought that a point tends to be reached where unit costs begin to rise."[5] The reason for this phenomenon is not a settled point of economic theory, nor is the existence of these *dis*economies of scale always acknowledged within a relevant range of output. Watson writes:

5. Bain, *Price Theory*, p. 112.

Can a firm keep on indefinitely doubling its inputs and hence always doubling its output? Everyone seems to agree that the answer is no, that eventually there must be decreasing returns to scale. The real problem is to find the clear cause or causes. On this point there is no agreement, even on the theoretical issue. Some economists hold that the entrepreneur himself is actually a fixed factor—though all other inputs can be increased, he cannot be. He and his decision making are indivisible and incapable of augmentation. In this view, decreasing returns to scale is actually a special case of variable proportions. Other economists believe that decreasing returns to scale arise from the mounting difficulties of coordination and control as scale increases.[6]

At this point it suffices to note that if some inevitable tendency persists to cause increasing inefficiency of management and control as the firm's scale of operations increases, it could well result in increasing costs per unit of output. However, these increases, even if forthcoming, might be insignificant on a per-unit basis when spread over a huge output. And the scale of output which induces diseconomies of scale in most real-world situations may well be outside any relevant range for empirical observation. The concept of economies of scale is more salient for an empirical investigation of long-run average costs than the notion of diseconomies of scale. Although one should not reject the possibility that diseconomies of scale are real and relevant phenomena, the essence of the long-run average cost curve for the firm is returns to scale.

Microeconomic Theory and Higher Education

There are some conceptual difficulties inherent when applying microtheory to IHL. They arise because IHL

6. Donald S. Watson, *Price Theory and Its Uses* (Boston: Houghton Mifflin, 1963), p. 143.

1. Provide a service rather than a product
2. Are not technologically dynamic
3. Produce a service difficult to define or delineate as to quality
4. Perhaps should be looked upon as simply aggregates of many rather independent producing units
5. Are subject to little external pressure that would influence the nature and efficiency of operations

Each trait will be discussed in turn.

Microtheory is implicitly addressed to the firm which is producing a *product* under the factory system. On the other hand, higher education is a *service* industry. It is not too difficult, however, to reconcile service industries with a classical microeconomics somewhat biased toward plants and firms producing tangible goods. This is especially true when the concept of economies of scale is of most interest.

As was noted above, the essence of economies of scale is found in the discontinuous factor of production. If all inputs in a particular process were perfectly continuous, there would be no economies of scale. Although it is a service industry, the "firms" in the higher education "industry" combine multiple factors to produce their "product." (The nature of this product is subject to debate, some of which will be presented below.) And, especially crucial for the application of the concept of economies of scale to IHL, the dominant input used in the higher education process, the teacher, is highly discontinuous.

The college teacher is a highly discontinuous input because higher education happens to be a service industry that performs several tasks in completing the product, and each task requires specialized personnel. For example, it is not normally the case that one individual is capable of instructing a college student in, say, both political science and biology. However, both of these tasks are necessary toward the completion of the final service:

imparting a liberal education. In addition, the specialized college teacher has a capacity such as 300 student credit hours per semester or some other such measure. Whether or not the institution has enough students to generate sufficient workload to meet the capacities of the specialized teachers is problematical. So IHL, utilizing discontinuous factors of productions, fit easily within the analytical mold of the economies-of-scale concept.

A characteristic of higher education which makes a direct application of classical microeconomic theory somewhat tenuous is the fact that IHL tend to be conservative in their use of non-human factors of production. This tendency was noted above (see p. 31), but it should be here observed that a firm without access to increasingly efficient real capital finds, as the scale of operations increases, a prime source of increasing economies of scale is foreclosed. This is not to suggest that higher education is completely devoid of any recourse to more efficient real capital as the scale of operations increases. But it is to suggest that IHL cannot, or do not, look to the use of more efficient hardware as a major source of decreased per-student costs as enrollments rise. This failure or inability to use increasingly efficient real capital, as output rises, stands, of course, in marked contrast to the firm of classical microeconomics.

The most perplexing problem facing those who would aspire to analysis of IHL, within the framework of the economists' traditional methodology, is the absence of a clear measure of work effort or result. Classical microeconomics takes as given a clearly defined unit of output measurable in both quantity and quality. However, able and honest men will differ greatly on the question of just what it is that IHL produce.

The obvious products of IHL would seem to be individuals who are more "educated" as a direct result of their participation in the academic programs. But it may be argued that defining a school's performance or output simply in terms of gross student attendance is insufficient, and that the student measure must, at minimum, be combined with an evaluation of the type of experience or environment created at the institution. That is, the measurement of performance or output at a college or university must go beyond measures of numbers of students and consider also the nature of the learning experience made available to the students. The demand that measurements of a school's output consider the nature of what is made available to students, as well as the number of students who avail themselves of it, is made by educators and generally placed under the heading of "interinstitutional differences in quality." In turn, there would likely not be as much desire on the part of educators to make interinstitutional differences in the learning environment an explicit part of the output measure of the schools if it were not for the interinstitutional comparisons that are common in much of the microeconomic analysis of higher education.

Thus, when one takes a school's total costs, influenced by both the number of students and the type of learning environment provided, and simply divides this total cost by the number of students to obtain a per-unit cost measure, he is missing much of the point. This is not to say, however, that there can be no meaningful objective measure of the nature of the learning experiences provided at one or a number of institutions. Interinstitutional microeconomic comparisons err when significant interinstitutional differences in learning environments are ignored. But it will be contended below that it is possible to make some evaluation of the probable differences in learning environments among IHL, especially to the extent that such differences would affect costs.

First, it may be safely argued that the majority of educators would likely contend that differences in total costs at two colleges, each with the same number of students and same objective mix of available learning experiences (for example, the same degree programs, distribution of academic disciplines, and percentage of faculty holding terminal degrees), and with the two schools being otherwise outwardly homogenous, are attributable to differences in quality. This is because there would be an implicit assumption that the school with the higher costs must be enjoying the use of resources of a higher quality, therefore leading to a learning experience of a higher quality. The incentive to accept such an assumption is strong, for to do otherwise leads to the conclusion that (1) there may not be a direct relationship between prices paid for resources and their quality in IHL or (2) there are identifiable differences in the quality of administration among schools. Both of these conclusions would be repugnant to those most intimately engaged in raising revenues and administering the expenditures of IHL. Be that as it may, one is unable to uncover the printed work of any reputable observer contending there is a direct, close, and positive relationship between costs and quality in IHL.

However, there are varying degrees of difference in the quality of learning experiences at various IHL, even when the programs appear outwardly homogeneous. But to attribute all quality variation to expenditure differences is absurd! There are many reasons for the varying quality of different learning experiences, and only one is the cost, monetary or real. To think otherwise suggests that an increase in expenditures for an academic program will, ipso facto, increase its quality or that two learning experiences which differ only in costs must have a quality ordering such that the low-cost operation is inferior to the higher-cost program. It can be argued that differences in the quality of learning experiences among IHL are much overrated in terms of their relationship to the program's costs. Thus, if enough care is taken to ensure that schools used in interinstitutional comparisons are sufficiently similar in terms of objective comparisons of academic programs and other learning experiences, the differences in total costs that exist may be largely attributed to differences in numbers of students served.

A more relevant argument against applying the economist's tools of microeconomic analysis to IHL is that the college or university is not the analytical equivalent of the firm. That is, it may be argued that some organizational subdivision within the school, such as the department or even the instructional section, is the most appropriate point for cost analysis. Robert L. Williams states, ''Cost studies to be meaningful should describe costs at each student level—freshman-sophomore, junior-senior, graduate or graduate-professional—for each department of each school and college.''[7]

Although this notion has much to recommend it, two observations may be offered: (1) collection of cost data at the level of the academic department or instructional section is not common today in American IHL and (2) only about 60–70 percent of total operating expenditures by a typical school would be charged to direct instruction. With respect to the first observation, to ask that all analysis be at the point of direct instruction is, in effect, to preclude almost any kind of analysis until accounting procedures used by IHL undergo major changes. Regarding the second point, indirect costs must be included in any analysis that purports to say something about the total costs of higher education. Thus, even if accurate and comprehensive data were available on the costs of direct instruction, exclusively, some arbitrary allocation of indirect costs would be necessary. Such a method seems to represent little improvement over collection of data at the level of the entire institution in the first instance, especially when there are to be interinstitutional comparisons, or use of data from many schools, in some kind of aggregate statistic.

7. Robert L. Williams, ''Instructional Cost Studies in Perspective,'' *College and University Business* 26, no. 3 (September 1955): 29.

Finally, microeconomic theory seems at odds with an industry composed of firms embracing various operational philosophies, and not in interfirm competition as such. The firm of the classical microeconomic model is subject to strong external influences, while American IHL are probably most subject to influences from within when actual decisions are made on factor combinations. The college has some discretion in deciding whether or not to adopt closed-circuit television; however, the local shoe shop has no choice whether a modern sewing machine will be used to attach soles. The relative isolation from outside influences, enjoyed in varying degrees by the many IHL, certainly makes interinstitutional comparisons somewhat risky. However, if care is taken to analyze institutions which are subject to some strong, homogeneous outside influences, interinstitutional comparisons and analyses may be made with some confidence in the results.

To summarize, IHL differ in both kind and degree from the firm visualized by classical microeconomics. The former is a service industry, producing a service difficult to define or grade, and with a static technology; it may well be only a collection of somewhat autonomous producing units; and it has considerable latitude in choosing factor combinations, as well as in other matters affecting operational efficiency. Nevertheless, IHL are not completely excluded from analysis using the tools of microeconomics. IHL still have the problems of discontinuous factors of production, and the degree to which differences in the quality of educational programs affect, or are affected by, costs may well be overrated. Analysis centering on departments and teaching levels does not improve on a gross per-student allocation of indirect instructional costs, so analysis of programs carried on at different locales might just as well consider costs at the institutional level. Finally, although institutions enjoy varying degrees of autonomy, it will be argued later that some are subject to significant and uniform influences from without, and these schools find some operational decisions to an extent forced upon them. It must be concluded that IHL are not as different from the firms of classical microeconomics as one might first suppose.

Costs of IHL: Some Broad Influences

IHL conduct various activities which, in sum, become the learning experience for the members of their respective academic communities. Each of these activities will be discussed in detail below, but here the discussion will center on two broad influences at work on all of these various activities to influence the level of monetary (but perhaps not real) costs. Although the analysis of the remainder of this study will be couched primarily in real terms, it will still be necessary to talk in terms of dollars, and any systematic influences on dollar costs demand some clarification.

A broad influence on the costs of IHL could be defined as a phenomenon which, ceteris paribus, results in consistent differences in costs among institutions. There are two broad influences at work on American IHL:

1. The relative abilities of IHL to raise operating revenue
2. The geographical region of the country in which the institution is located

The first should be so obvious as to require little explanation. All educational and noneducational institutions, public or private, must exchange liquid monetary claims for the economic resources they consume. One source of the considerable diversity in American higher education today is the varying abilities of individual IHL to acquire these monetary claims. There may well be American IHL which determine their expenditures budget free of any concern about revenues; but, if so, they must be extremely rare. The typical college or university finds planned expenditures and revenues converging, with the final level of each somewhat influenced by that of the other. One of the safest generalizations one can make concerning the expenditures of any college or university, for any activity, is that expenditure levels will be under the influence of revenue levels.

Because such a high percentage of the total costs of every activity conducted by IHL is for personnel,[8] one would expect that any broad influences on the general cost of labor in a locale would also have some effect on the IHL in the area. The United States does seem to be characterized by significant differences in compensation, for similar types of workers, in different geographical regions of the country. A few statistics will verify this observation.

Table 2.1 lists 1966 average wage and salary personal income, for the combined work force in service industries and state and local governments, in the various geographic regions of the United States. If wages and salaries in services and state and local government may be taken as a rough estimate of prevailing compensation levels for nonprofessional employees in higher education, it appears likely that substantial interregional variation exists for the latter. Table 2.1 indicates, for example, that average wage and salary personal income, for workers in services and state and local government, was about one and one-half times as high in the Far West as in the Southeast, and 43 percent higher in the former than in the Plains. Therefore, it is not unreasonable to posit that substantial differences do exist in the costs of nonprofessional personnel in IHL from one region of the nation to another.

However, teachers and other professional personnel account for the largest share of the personnel budget at the typical college

8. A typical school devotes about 70–80 percent of its total noncapital expenditures to personnel expenses. This generalization will hold true for each broad classification of institutions.

TABLE 2.1

AVERAGE WAGE AND SALARY PERSONAL
INCOME, ALL EMPLOYEES IN SERVICES AND
STATE AND LOCAL GOVERNMENT, BY
REGIONS, 1966

Region	Personal Income[a]
Far West	$5,944
Mideast	5,376
New England	4,861
Southwest	4,490
Rocky Mountain	4,332
Plains	4,170
Southeast	4,026

SOURCES: U.S. Dept. of Commerce, Office
of Business Economics, *Survey of Current Business*,
August 1969 (Washington, D.C.: GPO) and
Bureau of the Census, *Statistical Abstract*, 1967
and 1968.

[a] Total wage and salary personal income
divided by total employees in the sum of
services, state and local government, and other
industries.

or university. Table 2.2 presents salient statistics on the behavior
of faculty salaries in the different regions of the country. It
suggests that a significant divergence exists in the probability,
from one region to another, that an institution will pay its
faculty, on the average, an amount in excess of the mean national
salary. For example, it is more than three times as likely that a
school in the Far West will have an average faculty salary greater
than the national average for all teachers than is the case for
institutions in the Rocky Mountain states. Also, the trend of
faculty salaries seems related to the trend of general economic
affluence measured by per capita personal income. When the
two variables in Table 2.2 were correlated using rank-order

TABLE 2.2

PER CAPITA PERSONAL INCOME AND PERCENT OF IHL WITH MEAN FACULTY
SALARY IN EXCESS OF NATIONAL AVERAGE, BY REGIONS, 1968

Region	1968 Per Capita Personal Income	Percentage of IHL with Average Salary above National Mean[a]
Far West	$3,879	33.3
Mideast	3,878	21.7
New England	3,771	28.6
Great Lakes	3,649	20.1
Southwest	2,982	20.0
Rocky Mountain	3,005	10.0
Plains	3,246	10.3
Southeast	2,682	11.2

SOURCES: "The Economic Status of the Profession," *AAUP Bulletin* 54, no. 2 (June, 1968) and Office of Business Economics, *Survey of Current Business*, August 1969.

[a] This column lists the percentage of IHL in the 1967–68 salary survey by the AAUP (institutions with professorial ranks except medical schools) in each region with an institutional average salary in excess of the national average for all personnel in the survey. Thus the average salary for about two hundred thousand full-time teachers in institutions with professorial ranks was $11,033; and, in the Far West, for example, one-third of all IHL in the survey had an institutional average salary greater than $11,033.

methods, the correlation coefficient was .7857. It would be expected that general economic affluence would stretch its influence to affect the IHL, and this does seem to be the case.

Thus, when all other influences on the costs of IHL are (it is hoped) identified, it will be necessary to recall these two broad influences: (1) the relative abilities of IHL to raise operating revenue and (2) the geographical location of the institution. It remains in this chapter to describe the activities of IHL, and to analyze and identify the influences on the costs of each.

The Educational Activities of IHL: A Description

Over time there has developed a standard system of financial accounting by IHL which allocates total noncapital expenditures to accounts or functions; these can also be called, in a broad sense, the activities of IHL. Two divisions are normally made. The first is a separation of total noncapital expenditures into (1) educational and general functions, (2) auxiliary enterprises, and (3) student aid. The second is a further subdivision into several parts of the educational and general category.

The latter two of the first division will be disposed of first, mainly because the present study concentrates on educational and general costs. The Higher Education General Information Survey, conducted annually by the Department of Health, Education, and Welfare, defines these expenditure functions in a succinct and, apparently, universally accepted manner.[9] Auxiliary enterprises are those activities which are a part of the institution's operations, but are not directly an educational and research program. Such activities include housing, food services, and book stores operated by the institution. Generally, these enterprises are self-supporting in the sense that no revenues from student educational fees, or from the general subsidy for the educational and research program, are devoted to auxiliary enterprises. However, it is not uncommon for these operations to yield a current surplus which is often applied to the education and general, student aid, or capital budgets.

Student aid generally includes monetary disbursements to students for which repayment or reimbursement in kind by the student is not obligatory. The grants-in-aid to performing athletes is a gray area, and institutional practice here seems mixed.

9. U.S. Dept. of HEW, Office of Education, *Instructions for Completing OE Form 2300-4, Higher Education General Information Survey, Financial Statistics of Institutions of Higher Education* (Washington, D.C.: GPO, 1966).

It should cause no concern for our purpose because student aid will not be subject to any analysis. It may, however, be noted that payment for services rendered to the institution by students (such as grading papers or teaching under an assistantship) should properly be considered an educational and general expenditure and not student aid.

The above mentioned survey lists nine functions within the educational and general category: (1) instruction and departmental research; (2) extension and public service; (3) libraries; (4) physical plant maintenance and operation; (5) general administration, general institutional expense, and student services; (6) organized activities relating to educational departments; (7) organized research; (8) other sponsored programs; and (9) all other educational and general.

Instruction and departmental research is, quantitatively, the most important educational and general activity, and "includes all resident (not extension) instruction and departmental (not separately organized) research in all colleges or schools and the administrative expense for operating these units." [10] The definition causes little difficulty except for the delineation of academic versus general administration. Generally, academic administration ends, in the organization chart, with the dean of faculties or some other such title. In many small schools, the responsibilities of some persons are divided between instruction and departmental research and other activities, and the personnel costs for such persons should be appropriately allocated.

Extension and public service includes all educational programs provided for *other than* resident students. There is some question concerning evening degree-credit courses, especially if they are provided by the school's extension division or a similar administrative organ. However, it seems most appropriate to consider such courses part of instruction and departmental research.

10. Ibid., schedule 4.

Libraries are charged with all expenses of operating their own general and specialized facilities as well as museums. It may be noted that the practice in collegiate accounting is to consider the purchase of library materials and permanent improvements such as binding to be current, not capital, expenditures.

Physical plant maintenance and operation often presents some accounting difficulties which arise from (1) the common costs associated with providing utilities to the total institutional physical plant, including auxiliary enterprises, and (2) an often thin line between maintenance and capital improvements. There is apparently much diversity among IHL in treating both of these, but it may be noted that the activity should embrace only the maintenance and operation expenditures for the educational plant.

General administration, general expense, and student services are debited with the expenses of the governing board and office of the president; of facilities used by all, such as the telephone switchboard or purchasing office; and of operations such as keeping student records and providing student health service. Often, this function is charged with all (or some portion of) the costs of indirect benefits for personnel whose salary expense is charged to some other activity.

Organized activities relating to instruction are those activities conducted as part of the program of instructional departments, but not considered direct instruction or departmental research as such. Intercollegiate athletics at some IHL fall in this category. Special activities organized by an academic department, such as a series of programs with outside lecturers, would also be charged to organized activities. Demonstration schools for the primary and secondary education programs would, likewise, be debited here.

Organized research includes separately identified and funded projects, with the exception of research centers funded by the federal government and other outside entities. The expenditure may or may not be reimbursed by a restricted research grant, but the research activity is separately budgeted.

Other sponsored programs are institutes or centers financed by an agency other than the school. In effect, it is a special educational research activity, but is financed from without. All other educational and general form a miscellaneous category for expenditures that are not logically allocable elsewhere. With this definitional discussion of the various activities of IHL completed, the subject turns in the next chapter to a theoretical model of the determinants of, and influences on, the costs of these activities among IHL.

Summary

The theoretical economic concept of economies of scale suggests that firms, with the ability to adjust the quantities of all factors of production, will realize declining per-unit costs of production to some point, constant costs for some range after that, and then, possibly, diseconomies of scale as the management of the firm is unable efficiently to coordinate at some large scale of operations. The output range characterized by declining per-unit costs, or economies of scale, is basically explained by the ability to make increasingly efficient use of discontinuous factors of production as the output level grows.

Higher education offers some formidable, but not insurmountable, barriers to the application of microeconomic theory. It is a service industry, but still utilizes discontinuous factors of production. Higher education is not technologically dynamic, but this only means the partial elimination of recourse to more efficient machinery as a factor in declining long-run per-unit costs. The output of IHL is difficult to define and grade, but a reasonably satisfactory answer may be found for it, and differences in the quality of the learning experience from one school to the next need not be closely associated with costs. There can be honest differences about the wisdom of using the institution as a point of analysis equivalent to the firm of microeconomics, but to put it aside seems a little idealistic at this stage of the microeconomic analysis of higher education. Finally, while it is true the typical IHL is not part of a competitive industry, there still are institutions subject to some highly pervasive and uniform outside forces, and these can be used for analytical purposes.

To initiate the development of a microeconomic model of the institution of higher learning, two broad influences on the costs of all activities at all IHL may be identified. First, each of the private IHL and the state groups of public IHL seem to differ in their ability to raise operating revenue. Such differences have an influence on the level of expenditures and, given that some activities of IHL seem to carry a little more priority than others, there will be an impact on the structure of costs. Finally, higher education is a labor-intensive industry, and the money costs of all personnel seem to differ significantly depending upon the geographical location of the school.

With the overview and preliminary theoretical characteristics of the American higher education microeconomic unit discussed and disposed of, we turn in the remaining chapters to the essence of this study: the theory, and empirical quantification of the theory, of per-student education and general costs in the long run. This necessarily breaks into two parts.

First, the observed, real-world behavior of colleges and universities must be converted, as nearly as possible, into economic principles. For in the final analysis, any empirical investigations must be supported by sound, a priori reasoning establishing cause-and-effect relationships between exogenous and endogenous phenomena.

Second, a rigorous empirical investigation must be undertaken to test, and support or reject, the reasoned principles. A priori reasoning and empirical investigation cannot be separated. Chapter 3 contains the former, and Chapter 4 is addressed to the latter.

3

Expenditures for the Core Functions of the Institutions of Higher Learning

This chapter combines some factual statistical data with logical inference toward development of a theory concerning the relationships between (1) expenditures for the core functions of IHL and (2) their various determinants. These core functions are (1) plant maintenance and operation; (2) libraries; (3) organized activities relating to instruction; (4) general administration, general expense, and student services; and (5) instruction and departmental research. In Appendix A a similar theoretical treatment is extended to (1) other sponsored programs, (2) organized research, and (3) extension and public service.

The five core functions or activities listed above are common to most colleges and universities, and, if one were to exclude organized activities relating to instruction, it would be rare to find an institution not regularly incurring costs for the remaining four core functions (plant maintenance and operation; libraries; general administration, general expense, and student services; and instruction and departmental research). Also, the core functions dominate most schools' total educational and general budget, typically representing between two-thirds and all of this budget.[1] More importantly, however, it will be seen that the

1. In the fiscal years 1957–58, 1959–60, 1961–62, and 1963–64 the core function absorbed 71.6 percent of total educational and general expenditures for all IHL (see Office of Education, *Educational Statistics, 1968*). Regarding the variation about this mean pattern of expenditures, financial data for approximately 500 IHL were gathered for various steps during the conduct of this study. A survey of

core functions are most sensitive to changes in some of the common quantitative characteristics of IHL such as the total number of students or the size of the physical plant.

Plant Maintenance and Operation

The operation and maintenance of the physical plant (hereafter called PM&O) is the most difficult to analyze of all the core functions because of the many influences on total function or activity expenditures. However, analysis is not impossible, and it may be facilitated if these manifold influences on total PM&O costs are classified and discussed under four broad headings:

1. The scale of the institution, measured directly in terms of the size of the physical plant, and indirectly in terms of total students
2. The mix and scope of the school's academic programs
3. The climatic environment and setting of the campus
4. Miscellaneous influences

PM&O costs are largely fixed in the short run, mainly because they are a function of what must be operated and maintained: the existing physical plant. This observation is self-evident. But as soon as the analysis shifts to a time period long enough to allow the size (and, as will be seen below, the nature) of the physical plant to vary, the PM&O costs become, indirectly, a function of those phenomena that influence the size and nature of the physical plant. The two most important determinants of the size and nature of the higher education physical plant seem to be (1) the scale or total size of the school measured in total

---

these data indicates that the overwhelming majority of all IHL spend between 65 and 95 percent of their total educational and general budgets on the core functions. Exceptions to this finding are, of course, present but rare. This survey is cited hereafter as *Budget Studies*.

students and (2) the mix and scope of the school's academic programs.

Just as it is self-evident that PM&O costs are a direct function of the size and nature of the physical plant to be operated and maintained, it should also be intuitively obvious that at least the size of the physical plant will be somewhat related to the scale of operations at the school, especially in the long run. That is, ceteris paribus, as total enrollments grow, the size of the physical plant must also usually grow. Of interest, however, is not only the question of whether the total number of students and the size of the academic physical plant are positively related, but whether the physical plant must grow proportionally to the increase in total students. A recent empirical study verifies that the size of the academic physical plant and total number of students tend to be positively related, and tentative evidence is provided to support a hypothesis that the academic physical plant must expand less than proportionally to the growth in total students.[2]

Data provided in this study allow computation of rank-order correlation coefficients between an independent variable, total students, and two dependent variable series: (1) academic building space and (2) a capital to enrollment ratio for schools in the same state using statistics gathered by the same agency.[3]

First, the size of the academic physical plant was correlated on fall term head counts for three different combinations of schools. The results, summarized in Table 3.1, suggest that, at least in this one state, larger enrollments are associated with larger academic physical plants and vice versa. However, it remains to examine relationships between the rates of increase in both students and the academic physical plant. Of course, if

2. Illinois Board of Higher Education, *State-Wide Space Survey: Fall Term, 1965* (1966).

3. Studies of building space must be handled carefully, especially if interinstitutional comparisons are to be made, because of the absence of standard definitions of space. For that reason, analysis of a single study is appropriate here.

TABLE 3.1

RANK-ORDER CORRELATION RESULTS: GROSS ACADEMIC
BUILDING SPACE ON FALL HEAD COUNTS, ILLINOIS IHL, 1965

Combination	Rank r^2
8 public universities	.95
16 public and private universities	.81
23 private four-year colleges and theological schools	.61

SOURCE: Computed from data in Illinois Board of Higher Education, *State-Wide Space Survey; Fall Term, 1965* (1966) pp. 80–81, 90–91.

the tendency is for the size of the plant to grow less than proportionally to the total number of students, the situation is one in which internal economies of scale are present.

Using the same data as before, the evidence is mixed on the relationship between the rates of increase in students and the academic physical plant. Again using rank-order correlation methods, a coefficient of .40 was obtained when a capital-enrollment ratio was correlated negatively on ascending measures of total students in thirty private colleges and theological schools. But the same methodology for seventeen public and private universities yielded an insignificant coefficient, .05. About all that can be said is that tentative but weak evidence exists to indicate that economies of scale may be present in the provision of academic physical plants as the school grows. In turn, a similar pattern for PM&O costs should result, in real terms, in the long run.

Different types of academic programs have varying requirements for physical plants on a per-student basis, and this will cause different PM&O costs among schools that are otherwise similar. Cartter, making calculations from data in the *California and Western Conference Cost and Statistical Study,* suggests that great variations exist in the space requirements, per full-time equivalent student, among the various broad disciplines.[4] On the basis of this study for universities, he calculated that agriculture required about twenty-two times as much area per student, for all purposes, as did social sciences or business. And the requirements for the latter two fields were exceeded about fivefold by (1) biology and (2) mathematics and the physical and engineering sciences. Thus, the relative importance of plant-intensive academic programs, measured in terms of their shares of total students, will cause quite significant differences in physical plant requirements among IHL, given some number of total students. Also, the differences in plant requirements among the various disciplines is most pronounced in the requirements for research space,[5] so the scope of academic programs will also have effects on plant requirements per student.

The diverse climate in the United States, of course, will result in substantial differences in the costs of temperature control and grounds maintenance in physical plants differing only in location, but this topic requires no further discussion. The setting of the school will also influence PM&O expenses; the costs of vandalism and security will likely be higher in a central urban setting.

Besides the effects of scale, mix and scope of programs, and climatic environment and setting, there are a number of procedural, administrative, and philosophical factors which will influence PM&O costs, either at some point in time or over the long run, and these make overall analysis of PM&O costs difficult. John Dale Russell and James Doi have listed some of these influences:

1. The design of buildings may neglect the maintenance factor, locking in high maintenance costs as long as the building is used.

4. Allan M. Cartter, "The Economics of Higher Education," p. 181.
5. Ibid.

2. Buildings costly to maintain because of age may be used past their useful life.
3. Expansion of a plant may be chosen in lieu of more efficient use of the existing plant.
4. PM&O staffing may be inadequate in either quantitative or qualitative terms; heavy use of students is an example of the latter.
5. There may be a failure to mechanize when it is economically feasible.
6. Purchasing practices may be uneconomical.
7. Equipment, tools, and hardware may not be replaced when necessary for lower overall costs.
8. Preventive maintenance may be neglected.
9. Capital improvements may be absorbing resources intended for operation and maintenance of the plant.
10. The members of the academic community may not be conscious of the problems of maintenance.
11. The philosophy of the institution may be to maintain the campus as a show place.[6]

In summary, there are diverse influences at work on total PM&O costs in real terms. The size and nature of the physical plant represent the major determinants of operating and maintenance costs; that is, the size of the school in terms of students, and the mix and scope of academic programs, will be crucial long-run influences on PM&O costs. There is some evidence that the size of the academic physical plant may decline on a per-student basis as total enrollments grow, but this evidence is far from overwhelming. When all other influences are considered, perhaps the following conclusion is most appropriate: There is

6. John Dale Russell and James I. Doi, "Analysis of Expenditures for Plant Operation and Maintenance," *College and University Business* 20, no. 2 (February 1956): 49.

little reason to expect the costs of operating and maintaining the academic physical plant to be a source of significant and continuing economies of scale as an institution's enrollments grow; on the other hand, there is no reason to expect these same costs to rise on a per-student basis over time as the school expands.

Libraries

It appears that total expenditures for libraries are divided into the following two elements based on the degree of rigidity or fixity: (1) the costs for professional personnel, which represent about 30 percent of total library expenditures nationally[7] and (2) the costs of nonprofessional personnel, materials, and operating the libraries, which seem to be rather closely related to the growth in total educational and general expenditures over time. But the most dynamic factor influencing library costs, in the long run, might well be the broadening and deepening of academic disciplines, with increasing demands they bring for additional library materials.

First, it may be noted that while degree-credit enrollments increased about 70 percent between 1955 and 1963, the professional staff in libraries grew about 47 percent.[8] This should not seem too strange because the nature of the tasks of professional library personnel in academic libraries (maintaining the collection, providing specialized assistance, supervising the nonprofessional staff) are not such as to be closely influenced by the number of students. On the other hand, the library share of total educational and general expenditures has been maintained at about 3.3 percent in recent years,[9] indicating that expenditures on other than professional personnel have generally kept pace

7. U.S. Dept. of HEW, Office of Education, *Library Statistics of Colleges and Universities, 1963–64* (Washington, D.C.: GPO).

8. See above, p. 16.

9. Office of Education, *Library Statistics*, p. 5.

with the trend of total educational and general expenditures. It may well be that the fixed element of total library expenditures discussed above will result in some decline in total library costs per student as the school grows. However, if the depth and scope of academic programs also increase over time as they have in the past, these actual economies of scale, by virtue of increasing enrollments, may be more than overcome by rapid increases in requirements for materials. This is probably what has happened in the near past, causing total library expenditures to remain a remarkably constant share of total educational and general expenditures.

A priori, one can posit that, ceteris paribus, a school should experience declining real per-student costs of libraries as enrollments grow, mainly because of the basically fixed nature of the professional staff and the primary materials collection. However, here the ceteris paribus assumption is unrealistic for real-world analysis of long-run library costs, because with a secular growth in knowledge and the accompanying increase in requirements for materials, aside from any consideration of the numbers of students, statistical per-student expenditures may well increase in the long run.

Organized Activities Relating to Instruction

Recent years have seen some developments that have diminished the quantitative importance of the accounting category organized activities relating to instruction. One development has largely removed intercollegiate athletics from the educational and general budget, and put it where it belongs—in a separate account to be considered much like a part of auxiliary enterprises. Also, there has been a drastic decline in the laboratory school, which formerly represented a major share of organized activities. In the words of one observer, John F. Ohles, "At the present time, some laboratory schools have been scrapped and most of the others are operating in a state of relative limbo, fearfully awaiting the ax."[10] Finally, the move to program-performance budgeting in state government has allowed teaching clinics and hospitals to now be included as part of a separate medical center account. And a similar status has been given to the farms and research facilities for the agricultural programs.

What remains in organized activities cannot be much related to anything specifically. In a survey soliciting fiscal information undertaken for other parts of this study, about one-third of all responding institutions listed no charges to such an account in 1967–68. It should be noted that when a college still operates a laboratory school and charges intercollegiate athletics to the educational and general budget, the determinants of such expenditures are probably something other than total enrollments. By and large, however, analysis of organized activities becomes a specialized study of medical, dental, agricultural, and pedagogical education, topics outside the scope of this study.

General Administration, General Expense, and Student Services

The costs of general administration, general expense, and student services (hereafter called administration) increased at a rate, during the 1950–64 period, of about 11 percent annually for all of higher education—about 45 percent faster than the rate of increase in expenditures for instruction and departmental research. Expenditure on administration was exceeded in the rate of increase only by spending for organized research during this period.[11] Much of the reason for this increase was alluded

10. John F. Ohles, "Is the Laboratory School Worth Saving?" *Journal of Teacher Education* 18, no. 3 (Fall 1967): 305.

11. Bureau of the Census, *Statistical Abstract, 1968*.

to earlier when it was noted the ratio of students to administrative professional personnel has been falling in recent years for both public and private IHL (see above, p. 37). Yet, in the recent past, while the average size of institutions has been increasing, it might have been supposed that administration costs, on a per-student basis, would have fallen because "the larger institutions tend to spend less per student for the administration and general function than the smaller ones spend."[12]

There are at least two explanations for this inconsistency. First, there is an element of incomparability in the time series data because recent years have seen a tendency for IHL to charge the employer's payments for staff benefits to the administration account, thus serving artificially to inflate data for more recent years. Second, there is still the matter of the declining ratio of students to administrative professional personnel which is the major cause of the rather spectacular increase in administration costs in the post–World War II period.

Here, the explanation could well be that more tasks are being performed in administration, independent of the change in the number of students. In short, whatever the nature of the function relating administration costs and the size of the institution, when the operations of administration are given, the function has *shifted upward* over time as administration has taken on more tasks. Put another way, it seems as if the several activities which are collectively called administration have been broadening and deepening over time, much as has been the case for the academic programs. It does seem possible, however, to isolate some activities of administration which are rather sensitive to the total number of students from other activities which would be considered fixed costs in any time reference.

12. John Dale Russell and James I. Doi, "Analysis of Expenditures for Administration and General Purposes," *College and University Business* 19, no. 6 (December 1955): 39.

There are some administration activities which could be expected to increase in absolute real terms as the total number of students grew. Depending upon the extent of automation in the student records office, costs here would be expected to increase with a rise in students. The registrar's office would likely require more assistance as enrollment applications increased. The dean of students and other activities extending personal services to students could be expected to increase cost activities as a result of growing enrollments. However, it might well be that the costs of services would increase more slowly than the number of students and, on a per-student basis, they would be falling. Such a decline would be attributed to an increasingly efficient division of nonprofessional labor, and the fixed costs of such professional staff as the registrar and dean of students.

In total administration, general administration and general expense dominate. One can think of no costs more fixed than, say, governing board expenditures. Per-student general administration and general expense should decline drastically as the number of students increases and, if cost increases are necessary because of a growing student body (as opposed to the addition of tasks), they should be extremely discontinuous.

Thus, it would be expected that administration, given the nature of operations, would be a *declining* long-run cost function on a per-student basis. Further, it would seem that it could be a most important source of economies of scale in the lower ranges of institutional size. For a school of 500 students with a president's personnel costs of $30,000, the cost per student is $60; however, increase this school to 5,000 students and the cost per student is $6. Since it seems reasonable to suppose the costs of administration are more fixed than any other educational and general function, the economies of scale in administration should be pronounced. It should, however, be cautioned that this conclusion assumes the operations of administration are fixed. Certainly, it appears this has not been the case in recent years as the operations of general administration and student services have been growing secularly in scope at most schools.

Instruction and Departmental Research

Instruction is the dominant activity of IHL, and any major trends in total institutional long-term costs will have to be largely explained here. And, instruction is composed of a number of separate cost elements, each of which behaves a little differently. These are (1) academic administration, (2) nonprofessional personnel costs (student or nonstudent), (3) instructional hardware, (4) supplies and materials, and (5) instructional personnel and associated costs such as travel. Each element will be discussed in turn.

Academic administration begins with the dean of faculties, or a similar office, and extends to any faculty member with a reduced teaching and research assignment owing to his assigned academic administration functions. It does not include teaching personnel committee work which is, more appropriately, an accepted part of instructional duties. It would be expected that, as the analysis moves up the academic administration hierarchy, the more fixed total costs would become. The absolutely fixed, of course, would be the chief academic administrative officer. Expansion of the total academic administration operation seems to come through a filling out of the lower ends of the chain, with a tendency for former teachers (who show aptitude for, or interest in, administrative functions) to be given full-time administrative assignments and be replaced by additional full-time teachers. It would seem the real costs of academic administration would be more a function of the numbers of programs and teachers, rather than directly related to the number of students. (Of course, the number of programs may be influenced by the number of students, while the number of students surely is the major determinant of the number of teachers.)

Thus, if one found two schools alike in all respects save the number of academic programs and teachers, it would be expected that the school with the greater number of programs and teachers would also have the higher real costs of academic administration. And, if one accepts as given the types of academic programs, one would anticipate that an increase in students would give rise to increased academic administration costs indirectly through the effect of the former on the number of teachers. Again, however, these costs should increase more slowly than the increase in students and decline on a per-student basis. Given the academic programs, academic administration costs are likely to be somewhat fixed, but not as much so as general administration or the professional library staff.

The requirement for nonprofessional personnel in instruction is a product of the recognized folly of having highly paid teachers devoting their attention to necessary but menial clerical tasks such as typing letters and filing. The total clerical workload seems to be most related to the number of teachers; thus it is indirectly a function of the number of students. This cost, in real terms, likely works out to some rough ratio of nonprofessional employee to teacher and is probably somewhat discontinuous. Given the relatively low salaries paid these persons, this is a minor item in total instruction, and even more so in the total institutional budget. Be that as it may, one would expect that any economies of scale realized in the costs of nonprofessional personnel in instruction would be exhausted at a rather low level of total teachers and students.

The requirements for instructional hardware can be quite significant in disciplines such as chemistry, and almost nonexistent in others such as economics. In disciplines where academic hardware is a function of the numbers of students in a particular program (such as biology and chemistry, requiring laboratories), as the physical facilities are expanded to meet increasing enrollments, per-student expenditures should decline some in the long run. However, if enrollments in programs using hardware are growing at a rate significantly different from that of the whole institution, all-school per-student costs might fall greatly or rise. Again, academic hardware is usually insignificant in relation to the total institutional budget, and its stock is often buttressed when there is a windfall increase in the operating budget, or when new physical facilities are constructed. One would not look to academic hardware in a search for a dynamic element in the institutional budget.

Supplies and materials deserve no great attention. It may simply be noted that these costs are a function of the number of teachers and, indirectly, students. Therefore, there is likely to be little variability on a per-student basis.

Teaching personnel costs will typically absorb about one-half of the total institutional educational and general budget.[13] As was pointed out above (see pp. 55–57), the geographic area of the country and the level of the institution (university, four-year college, junior college) seem to exert the most influence on a per-teacher basis. On a real basis, teaching personnel per student appear to be a function of (1) the level of the institution defined in terms of the quantitative impact of graduate and professional studies, (2) the planned maximum student-teacher ratio in each instructional program, (3) the ratio of lower-division to upper-division students, and (4) the mix of disciplines in the institution defined in terms of each discipline's share of total students.

Graduate and professional courses are typically smaller than undergraduate classes in the same disciplines. This is because of the heavy reliance on the seminar method in graduate courses, and the fact that in only the largest schools are the graduate

13. *Budget Studies.*

programs of most departments large enough to allow instructional sections of a reasonably efficient size. Thus, all else equal, a school will find that the student-teacher ratio creeps down as the ratio of graduate to undergraduate students increases. This is not to make any judgments about the pedagogical methods of graduate instruction—it is only to note a real phenomenon.

The most important influence on per-student real teaching personnel costs, and thus the major determinant of the nature of the long-run cost function for the entire institution, is the institution's *planned maximum student-teacher ratio*. For when this ratio has been realized, the school will be at (or fast approaching) a total number of students which will allow annual increments to the teaching staff in a *constant ratio* to the annual increment in students. In short, the school staffs its academic departments at some threshold level, and total students increase annually until this threshold level stands in such a relationship to total students that *additional students will induce the institution to add to its faculty.* If, when this threshold faculty has been filled out by the growth of the school and the normal annual increment in students is equal to or larger than the planned maximum student-teacher ratio, then the average student-teacher ratio will become constant over time. An example will serve to illustrate this principle.

Assume a four-year school commences operations in year 1 offering a B.A., and the following policy decisions are made:

1. Proper breadth and depth in this B.A. program requires at least fifteen different academic departments with an average of two teachers in each department; in effect, a minimum of thirty teachers is needed for the program, regardless of how few students there are in total.

2. The school should not allow the institution-wide student-teacher ratio to exceed 20 to 1 because it might result in an excessive workload for the teachers and some teaching sections

that would be too large, both working to the detriment of the quality of the B.A. program.

This hypothetical school must grow to 600 students, at minimum, to push the institution-wide student-teacher ratio to the planned maximum of 20 to 1. It may take a few or many years, depending upon factors which are not of interest here. The important point is that if costs are expressed in terms of teachers per student (the reciprocal of the student-teacher ratio), the function relating costs and students would assume the shape of a *rectangular hyperbola* over the range 0–600 students. The reason, of course, is that the thirty teachers represent a *fixed cost* until the school grows to 600 students.

When the school has reached and is growing past the 600-student mark, the teaching staff must be expanded to prevent the actual student-teacher ratio from exceeding the planned maximum student-teacher ratio. If the annual increment is, say, forty students, the addition each year of two more teachers will keep the actual and planned maximum student-teacher ratio in balance. Thus, the cost function relating teachers per student and total students now becomes *constant* for any number of students in excess of 600. As the threshold faculty of thirty teachers is being filled out by growing enrollments, the cost function relating teachers per student and total students is a rectangular hyperbola equivalent to the economist's familiar short-run average-fixed-cost function; once the school grows to a point which allows the threshold faculty to be utilized at the student-teacher ratio representing the planned maximum, the growth in students and in faculty proceeds in a constant ratio equal to the planned maximum.

The real world will not, of course, run as smoothly as this abstract model, but the principle does seem to be at work.[14]

14. This principle will be offered as the explanation for the lower student-teacher ratios that may be observed among the smaller schools of any type. See Chapter 4.

The total range over which threshold staffing is being filled out, and per-student costs are falling most rapidly, will be the range over which *per-student costs of the entire school* are falling most spectacularly. Of course, it is apparent this range is given by (1) the level of threshold staffing and (2) the planned maximum student-teacher ratio. The greater the threshold staffing and planned maximum student-teacher ratio, the wider the falling per-student cost range. It is apparent also that each of these decisions will be due to institutional and departmental philosophies, with the all-school student-teacher ratio becoming a weighted average of the individual departments' student-teacher ratios. Further, it is obvious that the largest departments in the institution will exert the most influence on the institution-wide student-teacher ratio and the point at which the threshold faculty is filled out. When the institution-wide student-teacher ratio is falling markedly over time, as the student body is increasing faster than the total faculty, the school will be realizing its most significant economies of scale. When the annual decline in the all-school student-teacher ratio ceases, the institution will have approached, for all practical purposes, the point at which all significant economies of scale have been obtained.

A final word about threshold staffing is in order. Because IHL typically receive some fraction of their total operating revenue from student fees,[15] it is unlikely that a new school will be actually able to establish threshold staffing initially at the level it would find reasonably proper—the revenue that it is feasible to raise from student fees is not closely related to what is needed per student. Thus, it would be logical to expect such schools to grow into threshold staffing, so to speak, as students and student fee income increase. The effect would flatten the theoretical rectangular hyperbola, but would not affect the point at which the average student-teacher ratio becomes constant. In effect,

15. See above, p. 39.

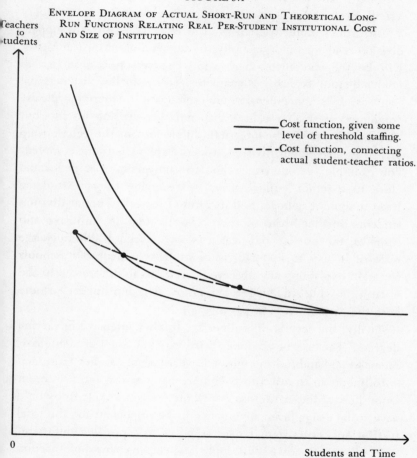

FIGURE 3.1

ENVELOPE DIAGRAM OF ACTUAL SHORT-RUN AND THEORETICAL LONG-RUN FUNCTIONS RELATING REAL PER-STUDENT INSTITUTIONAL COST AND SIZE OF INSTITUTION

Teachers to students

——— Cost function, given some level of threshold staffing.

– – – – Cost function, connecting actual student-teacher ratios.

0

Students and Time

if the actual student-teacher ratios were observed over time, one would see points on successively higher real cost functions merging at the planned maximum student-teacher ratio. Figure 3.1 illustrates this.

Institutions differ a little in the ratio of lower- to upper-division students, and generally the higher this ratio, the higher will be the student-teacher ratio. The reason is that just as graduate study typically is characterized by smaller instructional sections, so is upper-division undergraduate instruction typically conducted in smaller classes than is lower-division instruction. The factors making for inter-IHL differences in the relationship of lower- and upper-division students are varied and complex. For example, a four-year school or university that is located close to a junior college may, by receiving transfer students from the junior college, find its ratio of lower- to upper-division students smaller than another school's that is similar in all respects, but not located near a two-year school. Although the ratio of lower- to upper-division students is probably a minor factor in explaining any observed variations in different schools' institution-wide student-teacher ratios, it is appropriate to note here the phenomenon in passing.

Finally, the several disciplines are teacher-intensive in varying degrees. The use of academic hardware on a per-student basis seems to go hand in hand with a lower student-teacher ratio, and enrollments in the various programs may grow at rates different from those of the institution as a whole. It seems likely this would have to be a significant divergence to be important for the total institution's costs, but it may be noted as a possible influence.

In all, given some philosophy concerning threshold faculty staffing, the concentration of graduate students, the ratio of lower- to upper-division students, and the mix of students among the various disciplines, the real cost of teaching personnel per-student should first decline quite significantly as the school grows from a small size, then slow down in the rate of decline, and finally become constant when the institution has grown to a size allowing at least the major departments to add faculty each year in a constant relationship to an increased departmental workload measured in students. This pattern, combined with a tendency for academic administration costs to grow absolutely at a slower rate than students, should result in economies of scale in the costs of instruction and departmental research. The key question is, however, At what level of total students will the institution fill out its teaching staff? The answer to this will be the major factor determining the number of students at which the school will realize maximum total economies of scale.

Total Educational and General Activities

Each of the activities in the total educational and general budget has been discussed. At no turn was there reason to expect that, given some assumptions concerning the institutional philosophy, student and program mix, the type of library, the scope of general administration tasks and services provided students, the climate and setting of the campus, and policy concerning expenditures on organized research and extension and public service, per-student expenditures would not decline or remain constant as the student body grew. The expectations of the behavior of per-student long-run costs in higher education are much the same as classical microeconomics would suggest. As the level of students grows from zero, per-student costs will decline over some range of enrollments, then become constant, and perhaps at some point start to rise as diseconomies of scale set in.

In IHL there appear to be four major influences at work contributing to the declining costs as maximum economies of scale, in total institutional costs, are being realized. In order of likely quantitative importance, they are

1. The requirement for the institution to fill out threshold staffing in the academic departments
2. The fixed nature of general administration and general expense
3. Declining per-student academic administration costs over a significantly wide range of enrollments
4. Fixed costs of library full-time personnel

Once the teaching faculty has been filled out and the average student-teacher ratio becomes constant, the total costs per student should decline very little as enrollments continue to grow. The costs of teaching personnel represent about one-half of total expenditures of the typical IHL, and once these have bottomed out, most of the economies of scale are realized. Of course, items 2, 3, and 4 will still decline, but in the aggregate they cannot result in continued, significant declines in total per-student costs.

Summary

Plant maintenance and operation is apparently subject to the widest array of influences of any of the broad educational and general activities, but it seems probable that larger enrollments will result in a lower capital to enrollment ratio, and therefore lower real PM&O costs per student. In addition, the several academic disciplines are characterized by diverse requirements for per-student floor area, as well as having different space demands for the students at each of the three instructional levels. The climate and setting of the campus will also affect PM&O expenditures. And finally, poor management practices result in higher costs, especially for maintenance of the plant.

Libraries are characterized by a rather rigid cost element (the full-time staff), but the remainder of the library budget is related somewhat to the level of students, but perhaps more so to the depth and breadth of the academic programs. To the extent that fixed costs for full-time staff dominate the total library budget, there should be some decline in total library expenditures as enrollments grow, given the type of library.

Organized activities relating to instruction have been declining in relative importance when the total educational and general budget is considered. The activities that remain in the category are mainly related to the specialized education of doctors, dentists, primary and secondary school teachers, and agribusiness-men, and will be most influenced by enrollments in these programs.

General administration, general expense, and student services have been increasing in cost in recent years at a rate second only to organized research. The main reasons for this seem to be the rapid proliferation of general administrative responsibilities and services to students. Given these factors, however, this aggregate activity is rather fixed in absolute cost terms, and should decrease on a per-student basis fairly rapidly in the low ranges of student enrollments. In fact, the economies of scale to be had, as a result of fixed general administration and general expense expenditures, will be of a major magnitude when viewed from the context of the entire institution.

Instruction and departmental research is the dominant cost activity in the entire educational and general budget, and as this activity goes, so will go the entire institution. The two primary cost elements in instruction are (1) academic administration and (2) teaching personnel and associated costs. The former seems to be a function of the scope and number of academic programs and the size of the teaching staff. To the extent these latter phenomena are influenced by total enrollments (and the size of the teaching staff surely is), academic administration will be influenced by the numbers of students. The nature of this relationship should be such that costs of academic administration per student decline some as total enrollments grow, but not as sharply as does general administration.

The large item is, of course, teaching personnel costs. The type of school will have an impact on real teaching personnel cost per student, this being higher in the university because of the significant amount of graduate study, and higher in four-year than two-year colleges because of the tendency for upper-division classes to be smaller than lower-division sections. The several academic disciplines differ in teacher-intensity, so the mix of students by field of study from one school to another will influence these real teacher costs.

However, given the type of institution, distribution of students among the three levels of study, and a similar mix of students by disciplines, the institution will experience an increasing student-teacher ratio over some range of students, which means declining real teacher costs per student. The reason is that there must be some minimum level of threshold staffing, and it will be a fixed cost until the student body has grown to the point that allows annual increments of students to be matched with annual additions to the faculty in a constant ratio of students to teachers. The threshold level will differ among schools and disciplines. But given the point at which the teaching staff is filled out by the total enrollments, full economies of scale will be exhausted.

Looking at all these factors together, there should be little doubt that, given some assumptions fixing an institution's role, per-student costs will behave in the long run much as micro-economic theory would suggest. The most dominant elements in the declining cost state will be (1) the growth of the school to where threshold staffing has been filled out to the planned maximum student-teacher ratio, (2) the fixed costs in general administration and general expense, (3) the declining per-student costs of academic administration, and (4) the fixed costs of full-time library personnel. Although some further declines in total per-student costs may be expected past the enrollment point which brings the threshold faculty to the planned maximum student-teacher ratio, they will be minor. In effect, the economies of scale in the real costs of teaching personnel will dictate, to a large extent, the nature of economies of scale for all costs.

With this theoretical discussion of the microeconomics of higher education completed, it is time to turn to an empirical testing of the theory as it applies to total educational and general costs (with adjustments to be noted). A final chapter examining the implications that seem to flow from this theory will follow.

4

An Empirical Test of the Theoretical Long-Run Cost Function for Institutions of Higher Learning

This chapter is devoted basically to an attempt to give empirical meaning and quantification to the theoretical model developed in Chapter 3. The previous studies of long-run, noncapital costs in higher education (which are presented in Appendix C) suggest a cost curve shaped much as the analysis of Chapter 3 indicates. Although these studies prove a little more subjective than is desirable, their primary shortcoming is that they do not encompass the range of institutional sizes found in American higher education today. Thus, the empirical study presented in this chapter will, if nothing else, supplement the previous work using current data.

The discussion of the empirical study in this chapter is in three main parts. First, the rationale and composition of the study are discussed. Then, the results, or the estimation of the quantitative nature of the cost function, will be presented. Finally, the relevance of the developed cost function for all institutions of a particular type will be examined.

Rationale and Composition of the Study

The attempt to quantify the theoretical long-run cost function for IHL developed in Chapter 3 is presented once more in summary form. Appendix B contains a more detailed and technical discussion of the composition and statistical methodology of the study, while the present goal is to give an overview of the manner in which the statistical study was conducted, the logic behind it, and the results.

In the Introduction it was stated that a goal of this study would be quantifying the functional relationship between the size of school and cost per student. The process involved the use of secondary data and a mail questionnaire to get financial data, designed for other purposes, and using these data to quantify the long-run cost function for a "typical" institution of higher learning within the framework of classical microeconomic theory. The first necessary decision concerned the type of statistical study to be chosen for the project, and the decision was made to use a cross-section study of one year's data, rather than to analyze time series data.

This choice of the cross-section approach was motivated by a desire to capture the essence of the classical long-run cost curve which (1) is in constant money terms and (2) assumes a given state of technology. Higher education has been characterized in recent years by rapidly changing money costs for factors of production, especially for professional personnel. For example, between 1960 and 1967 the mean nationwide average salary for ranked faculty in IHL increased about 54 percent; during the same period, mean compensation for all employees in the private sector was rising about 31 percent.[1] Thus, the use of time series data of IHL to develop a long-run cost curve would require some deflation of money costs, and would have to go far into the past to accumulate a series with a range of institutional size useful for this study. And, although the state of the technology in higher education has not changed much in centuries, the individual

1. Computed from data in "The Economic Status of the Profession," *AAUP Bulletin* 54, no. 2, June 1968 and Office of Business Economics, *Survey of Current Business*, July 1968. The variable "mean compensation for all employees in the private sector" is basically the annual total payrolls divided by annual FTE employees.

school has changed in the recent past as the nature and types of academic programs have been modified and expanded, as the tasks of general administration have been enlarged, and as the services extended to students have changed in both depth and breadth. Time series data on IHL, to be used to meet the assumptions of the classical long-run cost curve, would require adjustments and modifications which would detract from the objectivity of the analysis. On the other hand, a cross-section study, although possessed of limitations that are discussed in detail in Appendix B, does hold constant the money prices of factors and the types of operations.

Once it was decided to use the cross-section approach, the problem was to determine the composition of this cross section. The theoretical analysis suggests inter-IHL comparisons and other analyses should hold constant (1) the abilities of the IHL to raise operating revenue; (2) the geographical location of the schools if one is forced to use money quantities in place of real quantities of factors; (3) the type and scope of acedemic programs, as well as general administration operations and services provided to students; and (4) the intra-IHL distribution of total students among the broad fields of study and the levels of instruction within each field.

Appendix B presents the rationale for the decision that groups of state-supported, four-year colleges within individual states best fit the above requirements. Private institutions are anything but homogeneous in their abilities to raise operating revenues, and this ability is the most crucial consideration in inter-IHL analysis. The other two alternatives were to use (1) public universities or (2) public junior colleges. Both were rejected as inferior to the choice of public, four-year, state-supported colleges.

Only four states have enough university campuses to allow a reasonable cross-section study, and conditions of IHL revenue-raising abilities differ enough among states to caution against combining, in one cross section, universities from more than one state. Also, intra- or interstate, public universities exhibit a great deal of diversity in the breadth and scope of academic programs and the distribution of total students among the various programs. Much of the diversity is likely the result of the early establishment of separate technological land-grant universities and "academic" state universities, although the differences in the two types of universities are generally narrowing over time. But at this point, it was felt there would be insurmountable obstacles to classifying a group of public universities differing largely only in the total number of students.

The use of public junior colleges also has shortcomings. First, the public junior college plays a specialized role that seems to be much affected by alternative educational opportunities in the general geographic area; so even within a state, one would not consider the community colleges to be homogeneous in a functional sense. Second, and most important, financing of the community colleges within a state seems to differ somewhat, with the assessed wealth of the school district appearing to be most crucial. However, data for two states with systems of state-supported junior colleges were available, and the analysis of these data is presented in Appendix D.

With the composition of the cross section determined, the study proceeds to uncover the national consensus among those making decisions concerning the allocation of revenues toward the operation of public four-year colleges. The consensus involves the proper relationship between per-student revenues or expenditures and the total number of students, when the institutions are homogeneous in all respects but total students, and the only remaining differential influence on total revenues or expenditures is the size of the institution. In short, the cross-section study attempts to discern the long-run cost curve for

IHL, *holding constant all influences on costs except scale.* The study does not attempt to derive normative information concerning the level of revenues to expenditures of IHL, but rather seeks out the *relationship between these financial phenomena and the size of the institution,* taking the adequacy or inadequacy of the level of monies simply as a given.

Since this study was to examine the actual relationship between per-student costs and the size of institution, it was desirable to study a model state (if such a determination could be made), or in the absence of such a thing as a model state, examine this long-run cost curve in states across the country. A model state was not uncovered because the expert judgments about state systems of four-year colleges seem to be most concerned with the level of expenditures, not the inter-IHL cost relationships. Therefore, the study of *thirteen* state systems of four-year colleges was undertaken, and the details of the selection and composition of this group are presented in Appendix B. At this point the geographical distribution of the thirteen states may be examined to demonstrate the national nature of the sample. By national geographic area, the thirteen states were distributed as follows:

Far West	2 states
Southwest	2 states
Plains	2 states
Great Lakes	2 states
Southeast	3 states
Mideast	1 state
New England	1 state

The theoretical discussion of the determinants of the costs of various activities suggested that organized research, other sponsored programs, and extension and public service expenditures were little related to the number of students in a school.

Public four-year colleges tend to debit these accounts only rarely and, when this does occur, by insignificant amounts. But in this study, any charges to the three above mentioned accounts were first subtracted from the school's total educational and general expenditures before this new figure was reduced to a per-student basis, using full-time equivalent students, a concept explained fully in Appendix B. Thus, this study is concerned with *adjusted* educational and general costs per FTE students.

The final item of interest in the composition and rationale of this study was the planned maximum student-teacher ratio in each state (when there was such a system-wide phenomenon) because this is the *prime* determinant, along with threshold

TABLE 4.1

FORMULAS FOR STAFFING STATE-CONTROLLED FOUR-YEAR IHL: THIRTEEN SUBJECT STATES, 1967–68

State Number	Formula for Student-Teacher Ratio
1	Lower-division approx. 21.6; upper-division approx. 14.4; graduate approx. 8.6
2	None formalized
3	All levels 16.0
4	None formalized
5	Lower-division 22.0 and 21.0; upper-division 18.0 and 16.0; graduate 12.0
6	All levels 21.0
7	None formalized
8	Lower-division 28.0; upper-division 20.0; graduate 12.0
9	Lower-division 21.5; upper-division 16.0; graduate 10.0
10	None formalized
11	All levels 20.0
12	None formalized
13	Undergraduate 18.0; graduate 10.0

SOURCE: Questionnaire.

staffing, of the shape of the long-run cost curve for IHL. As an indicator of institutional philosophies, the states from which data were obtained were also asked to describe any instructional staffing ratio used by their state-controlled schools for budgetary purposes, or by any other public bodies (such as a coordinating council or legislature) for providing this budgetary support. The results of this survey are presented in Table 4.1.

When it is considered that most four-year colleges typically find more than one-half of their students and instructional workload in the lower division, a rough average of the data in Table 4.1 indicates a tendency for the planned maximum student-teacher ratios to approximate 20.0. State number three budgets undergraduate instruction at considerably below this, 16.0, while state number eight seems to exceed 20.0 by about 25–30 percent, depending upon the distribution of lower-division and upper-division students in the schools. Except for these extremes, the concentration in the 18.0 to 20.0 range is marked.

Estimation of a General IHL Long-Run Cost Function

The analysis of Chapter 3 suggests that, given ceteris paribus assumptions concerning the type and revenue-raising abilities of IHL, there is a theoretical function which will explain the behavior or real noncapital costs per student as the size of the institution changes. A major goal of this study is to make an estimate of this theoretical function which will be called the four-year IHL long-run cost function (or general function). We do not wish to suggest that a cost function for four-year schools can be confidently used for universities or junior colleges. The matter of the applicability of a function, derived from public IHL data, to private IHL of similar types will be discussed shortly. The purpose of this section is to describe briefly the manner in which this general function was estimated and to focus on the results.

A detailed explanation of the statistical methodology appears in Appendix B.

The derivation of the general function, once the composition of the study had been established, involved (1) fitting parabolic functions of the general form

$$y' = a + bx + cx^2$$

(where y' is expected per-student cost; x is the school size measured in FTE students; and a, b, and c are regression coefficients) to 1967–68 data for each of the thirteen subject states and (2) making from these *intermediate* cost functions, an estimate of the expected function for a group of similar four-year colleges, where the only influence on total expenditures was the number of FTE students. The general function could be considered a consensus of the conventional wisdom concerning the allocation of revenue to various-sized state-supported four-year colleges in the thirteen subject states. But it may also be labeled the growth path of a school in real terms, given the ceteris paribus assumptions discussed above.

The expectations of the shape of a long-run average-cost function for IHL would suggest a parabolic function convex to the abscissa when FTE students is the variable on that axis. In Table 4.2 the constants and coefficients for the intermediate functions are presented with indices of correlation and determination. Table B.2 in Appendix B compares, for each state, the value of the index and coefficient of determination, thereby testing the superiority of a parabolic function in fitting the same data. Figure 4.1 shows the geometric representation of each of the thirteen parabolic intermediate functions.

First, in all thirteen cases, the parabolic function fitted by least-squares was convex to the abscissa when FTE students is the variable on this axis; the analysis of Chapter 3, of course, indicated the same for the theoretical function, and a curve of this

TABLE 4.2

INTERMEDIATE AVERAGE-COST FUNCTIONS: THIRTEEN SUBJECT STATES

State Number	Index of Correlation	Index of Determination	a	b	c
1	.9074	.8233	$2,240.76	−0.1590	0.000005410
2	.7750	.6006	1,331.79	−0.2020	0.000034200
3	.7110	.5055	1,054.98	−0.1600	0.000015400
4	.8329	.6937	2,061.23	−0.1690	0.000008050
5	.9796	.9596	1,978.61	−0.2960	0.000021500
6	.9516	.9054	1,252.53	−0.2040	0.000024000
7	.6544	.4283	1,166.77	−0.0452	0.000002450
8	.8865	.7858	1,135.26	−0.1960	0.000016200
9	.9640	.9294	1,266.16	−0.1450	0.000013400
10	.7529	.5668	1,282.70	−0.0897	0.000006350
11	.7479	.5593	1,251.59	−0.0399	0.000000696
12	.6701	.4490	981.19	−0.0316	0.000000593
13	.7781	.6054	1,376.34	−0.0930	0.000003150

SOURCE: Computed from questionnaire data.

shape is also the representation of the classical long-run average-cost curve for the firm. Second, in all thirteen cases a parabolic function was superior to a linear function in explaining interinstitutional variation in per-student expenditures. Third, as both Table 4.2 and Figure 4.1 illustrate, the intermediate parabolic functions differ more in position than in shape; that is, the ordinate intercept is more crucial than the x and x^2 coefficients for explaining noncoincidence of the intermediate functions. Fourth, Figure 4.1 also illustrates the general tendency for a lower index of determination for an intermediate function to be associated with a more shallow geometric representation of the function; the implication is that the sum of all influences other than size, on per-student costs among these IHL, is equalizing in effect. That is, the sum of all influences other than size tend to reduce differences in per-student expenditures. Fifth, the values

FIGURE 4.1

INTERMEDIATE COST FUNCTIONS, THIRTEEN SUBJECT STATES

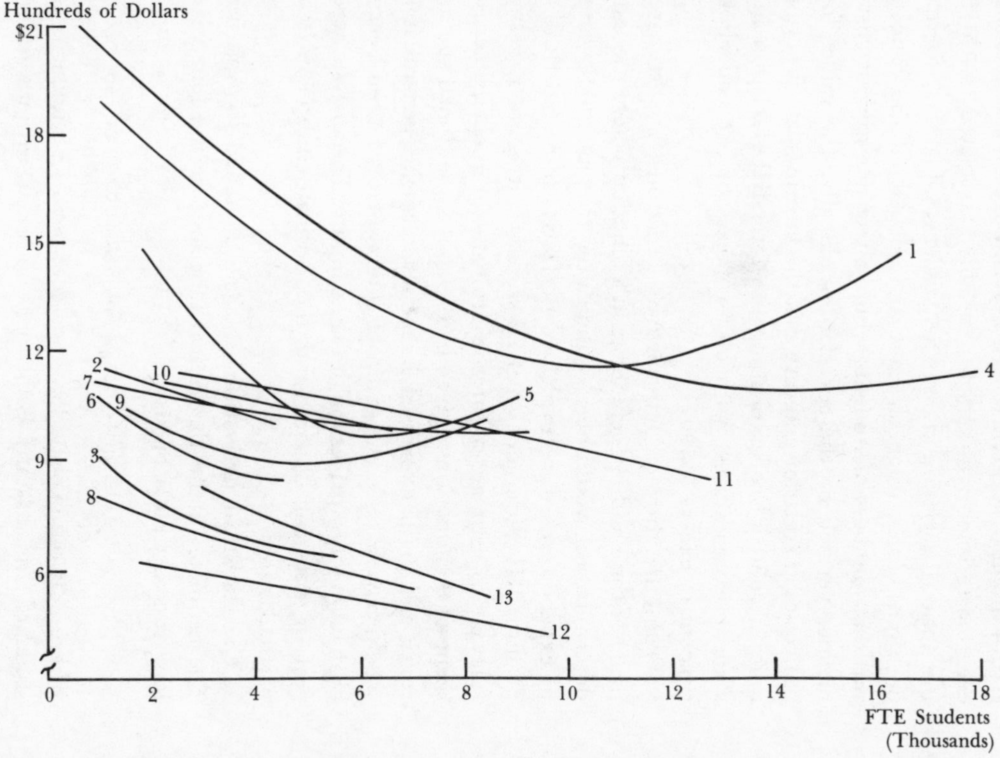

97

of the indices of determination indicate, in these states, that the size of the institution measured in terms of FTE students is by far the most important single variable associated with inter-institutional variation in costs per student. Of course, correlation does not, alone, establish cause and effect; but the expectation was that numbers of students would affect per-student costs in a manner verified by the correlations. Finally, the values for the indices of correlation indicate that the intermediate functions do quite a good job of explaining the inter-IHL variation in per-student expenditures, with all in excess of .65 and about 46 percent in excess of .80.

From the thirteen intermediate functions, an estimate was made of the x and x^2 coefficients in a function where the index of determination would be 1.0, indicating that inter-IHL variations in expenditures were explained perfectly, in a statistical sense, by inter-IHL differences in FTE students. It is not necessary or relevant to estimate a (or the ordinate intercept), because the shape of the function is given by the above mentioned coefficients (or b and c). If expressed in money terms, a general function would have a different ordinate intercept over time because of changing money prices for the same inputs. The analysis here is in real or constant dollars, and the ordinate intercept is of no particular interest.

The statistical derivation is, again, detailed in Appendix B. The estimate of the theoretical function, or the four-year IHL long-run cost function, is

$$y' = a - 0.244x + 0.00002275x^2 \qquad (1)$$

where y' is the expected average cost per FTE student, x is FTE students, and a is any assumed value for an ordinate intercept. This general function is portrayed in Figure 4.2 assuming a value of $1,500 for the ordinate intercept, and a schedule for the illustrated function is contained in Table 4.3.

Figure 4.2 and Table 4.3 indicate that maximum economies of scale are realized in a four-year institution of about 5,363 FTE students. (The analysis neglects the cost of real depreciation because most IHL do not keep depreciation accounts. However, per-student depreciation of buildings and structures has been estimated at about 2 percent of direct instructional costs, so real capital costs are not significant.)[2] Since a geometric parabola does not contain any linear segments, the linear portion in Figure 4.2 from 5,363 to 10,000 FTE students has been subjectively drawn to suggest a theoretical constant average-cost range. Of course, the objective value of the general function ends at the vertex (maximum economies of scale), and it is the shape of the function to 5,363 FTE students that is of most interest.

In the Introduction it was also suggested that, for the development of a general long-run average-cost function for IHL to be

TABLE 4.3

THE FOUR-YEAR IHL LONG-RUN COST
FUNCTION, ASSUMING AN ORDINATE INTER-
CEPT OF $1,500 IN 1967–68 DOLLARS

FTE Students	Annual Average Cost per Student
500	$1,383.69
1,000	1,278.75
2,000	1,103.00
3,000	972.75
4,000	888.00
5,000	848.75
5,100	847.33
5,200	846.36
5,300	845.85
5,363	845.75[a]

[a] Minimum cost.

2. Edding, "Expenditures on Education: Statistics and Comments," p. 42.

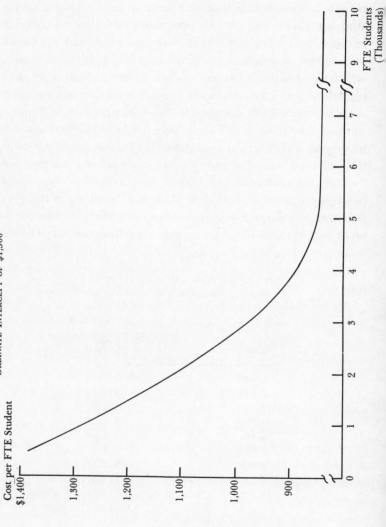

FIGURE 4.2

THE FOUR-YEAR IHL LONG-RUN COST FUNCTION, ASSUMING AN
ORDINATE INTERCEPT OF $1,500

Cost per FTE Student

$1,400

1,300

1,200

1,100

1,000

900

0   1   2   3   4   5   6   7   8   9   10

FTE Students
(Thousands)

of much moment, the economies of scale possible (if any) should be of substantial magnitude—this appears to be the case: Figure 4.2 and Table 4.3 indicate that an institution of 5,363 FTE students incurs annual costs per student of about $538 less than a school of 500 students. And the same school of 5,363 students will have annual per-student costs of about $433 less than an institution of 1,000 students. Such differences in per-student costs among IHL of various sizes are substantial by any measure. There seems to be little doubt that the general function should have more than just passing interest for those concerned with the allocation of resources to institutions of higher learning.

It should also be noted here that percentage differences in costs among IHL of various sizes have no meaning in the general function. For percentage differences are, of course, related to the level, not the shape, of the average-cost function. The absolute monetary amounts, reflecting absolute real costs per student (by virtue of using data for one pricing period, so to speak), are of interest.

Another item of analytical interest in Table 4.3 and Figure 4.2 is the range of school sizes in which the major portion of the relevant economies of scale are realized. With between 500 and 5,363 FTE students, the per-student costs decline about $538. More than three-fourths of this total decline has been realized by the time the school enrolls 3,000 students, and about 92 percent is enjoyed when the institution has attained the level of 4,000 FTE students. Recalling that most economies of scale will have been realized when threshold staffing in the academic departments has been filled out, and that a planned maximum student-teacher ratio in the thirteen subject states seems to hover about 20.0, one finds that the "typical" absolute level of threshold teaching faculty in state-supported, four-year colleges seems to be between 150 and 175 teachers. That is, in 1967–68 when a public, four-year college had covered all academic programs with

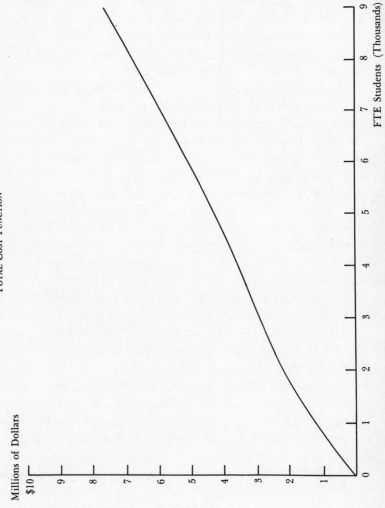

FIGURE 4.3

TOTAL COST FUNCTION

Millions of Dollars

$10
9
8
7
6
5
4
3
2
1

0   1   2   3   4   5   6   7   8   9

FTE Students (Thousands)

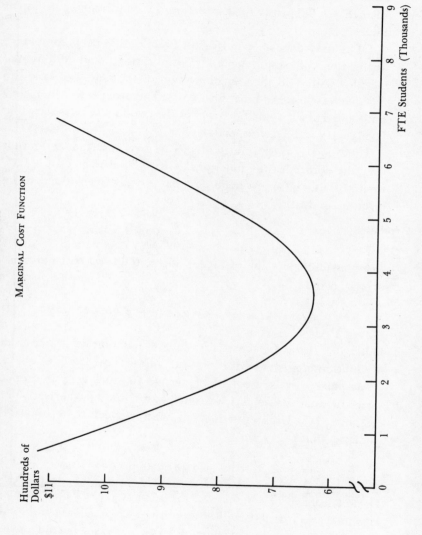

FIGURE 4.4

MARGINAL COST FUNCTION

from 150 to 175 full-time teachers, further additions to the staff seemed to be primarily a reaction to continuing enrollment increases.

Of course, once an average-cost function has been computed, application of some logic, multiplication, and differential calculus will yield the remaining two of the family of long-run cost curves—total and marginal costs. The process will be briefly outlined, and a graphic portrayal of the two functions is shown in Figures 4.3 and 4.4, respectively.

Total cost is the product of (1) average cost and (2) output over the domain of the functions. That is, if average cost is $f(x)$, total cost is $x \cdot f(x)$. Average cost has already been found to be given by evaluating

$$y' = a - 0.244x + 0.00002275x^2.$$

Again assuming a value of \$1,500 for a, the total cost function, or $g(x)$, would be

$$g(x) = \$1,500x - 0.244x^2 + 0.00002275x^3 \qquad (2)$$

indicating that total costs are zero when output is zero, an assumption consistent with long-run adjustment.

Marginal cost is the rate of change in total cost as output varies. If total cost is $g(x)$, marginal cost is the first derivative of $g(x)$ or $g'(x)$. Differentiating (2) with respect to x (or FTE students) yields

$$g'(x) = \$1,500 - 0.488x + 0.00006825x^2. \qquad (3)$$

The vertical axis of symmetry of (3) is about 3,575 FTE students. This indicates that IHL with fewer than 3,575 students find total costs increase less than proportionally to increases in students as the school grows toward 3,575 total FTE students.

Finally, the general function has upper and lower limits that require explanation. Basically, there are too few schools of less than five hundred students in the study group to examine the cost relationships in this range. In the thirteen subject states, two states each had one school of less than 500 FTE students in the fall of 1967; the two schools were simply excluded from the computation of the intermediate functions for those states. (Appendix B outlines other reasons for excluding a single school from the computation of the intermediate functions.)

In the upper ranges of FTE students, it appears that the schools assume characteristics somewhere between those of a four-year college and a university, although they are still classified officially as four-year schools. Basically, the reason is that the size of the four-year college and the ratio of graduate to undergraduate students are positively related. In turn, the school is influenced by the fact that its "market area" must be quite densely populated to yield enough potential graduate students to justify the high initial and ongoing costs of graduate programs. A few statistics will illustrate these observations.

Table 4.4 lists rank-order correlation coefficients obtained in each of the thirteen states when the ratio of graduate to undergraduate FTE students was correlated on total FTE students, ranked in such a way that a positive correlation coefficient would indicate a positive relationship between the two variables.

Obviously, there is some relationship between the concentration of graduate students and the size of the institution. In nine of the thirteen subject states, the rank-order correlation coefficient quantifying this relationship was greater than .6. One of the reasons for this relationship, as was stated above, is that large schools tend to be in densely populated areas which yield more potential graduate students. A sample of 240 four-year, state-supported IHL for fall, 1967, indicated that two-thirds of the schools of 5,000 FTE students or less were in rural areas

TABLE 4.4

RANK-ORDER CORRELATION COEFFICIENTS:
RATIO OF GRADUATE TO UNDERGRADUATE
FTE STUDENTS ON TOTAL FTE STUDENTS,
THIRTEEN SUBJECT STATES

State Number	Rank-Order Correlation Coefficient
1	.7532
2	.7610
3	< 0
4	.8061
5	.6191
6	.2000
7	.8114
8	.8500
9	.8000
10	.6612
11	.9429
12	.3882
13	< 0

SOURCE: Computed from questionnaire data.

(outside standard metropolitan statistical areas or in towns of less than 60,000 population); however, one-half of the schools with more than 5,000 FTE students were in urban areas.[3] Thus, it appears that statements about the costs of very large schools should not be made from this study, not only because there were relatively few such large schools in the subject states, but also because large four-year colleges appear to be unique types of schools. The general function is, therefore, limited to the range of 500 to 10,000 FTE students when strictly construed.

3. Computed from data in U.S. Dept. of HEW, Office of Education, *Students Enrolled for Advanced Degrees, Fall, 1967—Part A—Summary Data* (Washington, D.C.: GPO, 1968) and in *Opening Fall Enrollments in Institutions of Higher Learning, 1967* (Washington, D.C.: GPO).

Relevance of the Four-Year IHL Long-Run Cost Function for Private Schools

Correlation analysis using private IHL does not prove as fruitful as when systems of state-supported colleges are studied, because one cannot identify as homogeneous a group of the former as of the latter. But long-run cost functions derived by cross-section studies do suggest something about the cost path of a single firm. Thus, if the general function presented above has much meaning, it must be that it serves as an estimate of the growth path for some individual schools. Its applicability to state-supported, four-year IHL is obvious. But, as has been stated, its applicability to universities and junior colleges would be unwise. It remains to ascertain whether the general function is relevant for the private four-year college.

If this study accomplishes nothing else, it should caution against any generalizing about the "typical" college or university. And especially as concerns finances, it is unwise to generalize about private IHL. However, the general function is (in effect) in real terms, and if private schools do not differ radically from public IHL in real terms, then there is some basis for comparison.

Many similarities exist between private and public IHL. Individual teachers move quite easily between the two types of institutions, and no radical adjustment seems necessary. The organization of the entire school and individual departments does not differ much, if any, from public to private schools. And the curricula in the two types of IHL exhibit more likenesses than differences.

Other investigators of the finances of IHL, using inter-institutional comparisons, have not hesitated to study private and public IHL simultaneously. For example, Russell and Reeves's definitive study of higher education finances used a comingled sample of both private and public colleges and universities.[4]

4. See Appendix C, p. 159.

However, it is desirable to have a more objective basis for holding that similarities between private and public colleges are great enough to allow cost functions, calculated on the basis of data from public schools only, to be used to explain real cost behavior in private schools as well.

One basis for objectively comparing the public and private four-year schools is to examine the distribution of conferred bachelor's degrees by broad academic fields. If these distributions are similar, it may be posited that the distribution of students among these broad fields was, also, rather alike, and that a difference in the relative emphasis on the several broad disciplines is not at work influencing the institution-wide student-teacher ratios in the two types of schools.

Six broad academic disciplines (education, social sciences, business, English, biological sciences, and mathematics) account for about 90 percent of all bachelor's degrees conferred by American IHL. Table 4.5 shows the percentage distribution of the bachelor's degrees awarded in these fields in 1965–66. As can be seen, the major difference between public and private IHL in the distribution of academic emphasis, if bachelor's degrees

TABLE 4.5

PERCENTAGE DISTRIBUTION: BACHELOR'S DEGREES CONFERRED IN SIX MAJOR
FIELDS, ALL IHL, 1965–66

Field	All IHL	Public IHL	Private IHL
Education	33	38	24
Social Sciences	26	22	32
Business	18	17	20
English	10	11	9
Biological Sciences	8	7	9
Mathematics	6	6	6

SOURCE: U.S. Dept. of HEW, Office of Education, *Earned Degrees Conferred, 1965–66* (Washington, D.C.: GPO, 1968).

NOTE: The totals for each column may not add to 100 because of rounding.

conferred may be taken as an indication of such a distribution, is that social sciences and education rank quantitatively first and second, respectively, in the private schools, while this ranking is reversed in the public colleges. The trend reflects the traditional roles played by the two types of institutions, especially the role of public teachers' colleges west of the Alleghenies. However, there is evidence that costs per student for direct instruction in the two fields differ by not more than 30 percent, and when it is considered that direct instruction accounts for about one-half of total per-student costs, the total differential between costs for the two disciplines is not more than 15 percent.[5] Thus, it appears that public and private IHL may be similar enough in the distribution of students and teachers among the several broad disciplines to disregard academic emphasis as a major source of differential student-teacher ratios in the two types of institutions, of course holding constant the other factors affecting this ratio.

Besides the level of instruction and the distribution of students and teachers among disciplines embracing different pedagogical methodology, the other sources of variation in real costs per student are (1) differences in the size of schools, resulting in economies of scale being realized to a disparate degree or (2) a consistent difference in the ratio of students to real inputs, given the size of institution. If the latter is found not to be influential, differences in real costs per student between public and private four-year colleges will be largely attributable to that which causes such cost variations among public institutions only:

5. Numerous studies by state coordinating agencies, university offices of institutional research, etc. have been made pertaining to the costs of direct instruction in various departments and levels of instruction. Two of the best of these are the *California and Western Conference Cost and Statistical Study* and the *Analysis of the Scope of Courses Taught, Class Size, Teaching Loads, and the Instructional Salary Cost for the Regular Academic Year 1967–68 for Credit Classes at the University of Colorado, Boulder, Denver, and Colorado Springs Campuses* conducted by the University of Colorado Office of Institutional Research (1969).

differences in the size of the institution and the resulting abilities to realize economies of scale.

The tendency of public and private four-year colleges to differ in the application of real inputs per student, given the size of the institution, can be reduced to a problem of testing the application of personnel per student because of the labor-intensive nature of higher education. That is, if it appears public and private schools of the same size have about the same ratio of students to personnel, all the major factors affecting real costs per student (except scale) in either type of institution will have been found to be homogeneous. Two separate statistical tests were made to examine the question of whether public and private four-year colleges, with similar enrollments, employed significantly different numbers of personnel.

First, from data published by the Department of Health, Education, and Welfare for fall, 1966, it was possible to ascertain institutions' ratios of FTE students to FTE personnel for

TABLE 4.6

DIFFERENCE-IN-MEANS TEST RESULTS: STUDENT-PERSONNEL RATIOS, PUBLIC AND PRIVATE FOUR-YEAR IHL, FALL, 1966

FTE Students	Mean Private S-P Ratio	Mean Public S-P Ratio	Difference	Whether Significant	Significance Level[a]
Under 1,500	6.5	8.1	− 1.6	No	0.05
1,500–2,999	7.3	9.1	− 1.8	No	0.05
3,000 and over	7.5	10.0	− 2.5	No	0.025

SOURCES: Computed from data in Dept. of HEW, Office of Education, *Numbers and Characteristics of Employees in Institutions of Higher Learning, Fall, 1966* (Washington, D.C.: GPO, 1969) and *Opening Fall Enrollments in Institutions of Higher Learning, 1966* (Washington, D.C.: GPO, 1969).

[a] Two-tailed test.

both professional and nonprofessional persons. A random sample of these ratios was taken for both public and private, co-educational, four-year colleges; the sample schools were classified by FTE students, and the mean student-personnel ratio for each FTE student size category was computed. In each FTE student size category, the difference in the public and private IHL mean student-personnel ratios was submitted to the difference-in-means test. The results of this test are summarized in Table 4.6. Certainly, the difference-in-means test is less than conclusive; for example, the level of significance for the size category of 3,000 and more FTE students is too low for comfort. But at least there can be a tentative conclusion that public and private schools of the same size tend to employ about the same numbers of personnel.

The second test was much the same as the first with the exceptions that (1) data are for the ratio of FTE students to FTE teachers and (2) the manner of classifying the schools by FTE

TABLE 4.7

DIFFERENCE-IN-MEANS TEST RESULTS: STUDENT-TEACHER RATIOS, PUBLIC AND
PRIVATE FOUR-YEAR IHL, FALL, 1967

FTE Students	Mean Private S-T Ratio	Mean Public S-T Ratio	Difference	Whether Signifi-cant	Signifi-cance Level[a]
Under 1,000	13.4	14.9	−1.5	No	0.25
1,000–1,499	13.9	18.0	−4.1	Yes	—
1,500–1,999	14.1	19.4	−5.3	Yes	—
2,000–2,499[b]	—	—	—	—	—
2,500–5,999	17.1	19.6	−1.5	No	0.10

SOURCE: Computed from questionnaire data.

[a] Two-tailed test.
[b] Sample response in this size class too small and nonrepresentative.

students was modified slightly to see if the results would differ
from those of the first test. They are summarized in Table 4.7.

Two conclusions appear possible from these difference-in-
means tests: (1) in the size range where about three-fourths of
the private four-year colleges are found (less than 1,500 FTE
students), there appears to be no substantial difference between
public and private schools in either the ratio of students to all
personnel or the ratio of students to teachers and (2) although the
evidence is a little tenuous, the following hypothesis is supported by the data: public and private IHL of similar size, but
with more than 1,500 FTE students, tend to employ the same
number of total personnel. Although the evidence is by no means
final and conclusive, it does suggest an absence of major differences in the real teaching costs per student, given the size of the
school, between private and public schools specializing in four-
year academic programs. Such evidence is both intuitive and
empirical. It could be advocated that if it were possible to isolate
a group of private four-year IHL as strictly as the public schools
were delineated, the resulting least-squares parabola fitted to the
cross-section data of the former would not differ much in shape
from the four-year IHL long-run cost function. In short, in lieu
of strong evidence to the contrary, it may be suggested that the
general function, in both its theoretical and empirical formula-
tion, is applicable to *both* public and private four-year IHL.

Behavior of Separate Educational and General Activities

The theory of the behavior of total educational and general
costs was the product of the combination of separate analysis for
each of the educational and general activities. Thus, it would be
appropriate, if possible, to submit these individual activities to
the same type of empirical test as in the case of total costs.
However, such a method proves difficult for at least two reasons.

First, data by separate educational and general activity are not always obtainable, especially since the information is not always intended for public consumption. For the present study it was possible to obtain this type of detail for the majority of the thirteen subject states, but by no means for all. Second, and more important, the amount spent in total by a school is a rather incontrovertible fact; however, the portion of the total spent, say, for general administration, as opposed to academic administration, is what the school's accounting department says it is. Given these limitations, some cross sections were studied for each of the separate activities, and the results are presented in Appendix D.

Summary

A goal of this study was to develop a quantitative expression of the theoretical function relating long-run per-student costs and the size of an institution measured in terms of total students. Toward this end a cross-section study of adjusted educational and general revenues or expenditures per student, for all of the state-supported, four-year colleges in thirteen states, was undertaken. The cross-section approach was considered superior to the use of time series data, mainly because of rapidly increasing money costs for professional personnel in IHL. State-supported, four-year schools within a state were used as the basic study group owing to their superior, objective homogeneity, save for institutional size.

To the data for each state, parabolic functions were fitted by least-squares, and these intermediate cost functions were then used to estimate the four-year IHL long-run cost function. It could be described as the least-squares function forthcoming if the only influence on inter-IHL per-student costs was the number of students.

A thirteen-state study was undertaken because of the apparent absence of anything approaching a model state system of four-year IHL. The thirteen states were distributed across the nation, and in all respects seemed representative of public higher education. The expenditure item studied was what will be called adjusted educational and general expenditures, which can be broken down into educational and general expenditures minus organized research, other sponsored programs, and extension and public service. Finally, a study of budgetary formulas used for academic staffing in the various states showed a rather consistent tendency towards an institution-wide student-teacher ratio of about 20.0.

The computation of intermediate functions indicated that (1) a long-run cost function for state-supported, four-year IHL is traditionally shaped, (2) a parabola is superior to a linear function for explaining inter-IHL variation in per-student costs, (3) the states differ more in the *level* of finances than in the distribution of same among various-sized IHL, (4) the sum of influences other than institutional size tend to reduce differences in inter-IHL finances, (5) the size of institution is the dominant variable in explaining variation in costs per student among similar institutions, and (6) the trend of per-student costs in state-supported, four-year IHL can be closely approximated with use of a parabolic function.

The intermediate functions were used to estimate the four-year IHL long-run cost function. This function suggests that per-student costs decline over the range of 500 to 5,363 FTE students, and it would be expected that costs would be rather constant for a range beyond the point of least cost. The cost decline is significant, being about $538 per FTE student from 500 to 5,363 students, and about three-fourths of the total economies of scale are realized by the time the school has attained the level of 3,000 students. The range of analysis is limited to 500 to 10,000 FTE students, basically because there are few public four-year IHL of less than 500 students, and because schools of greater than 10,000 seem to assume some of the characteristics of a university, with a growth in the ratio of graduate to undergraduate students.

The question of the relevance, for private schools, of a function estimated from examination of public school data, should be faced. Many types of evidence, some more scientific than the rest, suggest there may be enough similarity between public and private four-year schools to render the conclusions, derived from the data for the former, valid for the latter. It may be observed that about the same academic programs are conducted at all four-year schools, and in roughly the same proportions. And a large sample of student-personnel and student-teacher ratios, at both public and private four-year IHL, revealed no significant differences in real teaching personnel costs per student in either the lower or upper ranges of enrollments in today's private liberal arts colleges. Thus, in lieu of evidence to the contrary, it seems at least a good bet that, if a group of private four-year colleges could be identified which were as homogeneous as the state-supported four-year colleges within a state, the least-squares parabola fitted to the former would differ little in shape from the four-year IHL long-run cost function.

Study of the costs of each of the educational and general activities is also in order, but it is complicated by a relative shortage of data and by the subjectiveness of accounting practices used to allocate total expenditures among the several activities. However, some cross-section studies of these individual activities were made, and are presented in Appendix D.

5

Some Concluding Observations

This final chapter will examine two broad subjects. First, a reconciliation is presented that bridges the difference between the quantitative expression of Russell and Reeves's IHL cost function (which is surveyed in Appendix C), and the general function presented in Chapter 4 of this study. In the process of the reconciliation, the durability of any general long-run cost function for higher education will be evaluated. To conclude the study, two important problem areas of contemporary higher education will be examined in light of the information provided by the four-year IHL long-run cost function. First, the current financial crisis of the private IHL will be appraised, given the implications of the general function. Finally, at the other end of the size range, the gigantic "multiversity" will be considered.

Reconciliation with Russell and Reeves and the Durability of the General Function

The conclusions of this study find areas both of agreement and disagreement with the landmark works of Russell and Reeves. The major area of agreement is that institutions of higher learning do, indeed, resemble somewhat the firm of classical microeconomics in that long-run unit costs first decline as the scale of output grows from zero, and then become constant for some range. The major area of disagreement concerns the range of institutional sizes over which per-student costs decline.

In their attempt to quantify the general relationship between per-student operating costs and the scale of the institution measured in FTE students, Russell and Reeves posited that

1. From 0 to 1,050 FTE students, the total costs of the school are constant or, put another way, the function for per-student costs in this range is a rectangular hyperbola
2. Above 1,050 FTE students, per-student costs are constant
3. The maximum size of school that their cost function might describe was 3,500 FTE students[1]

However, the conclusions of the present study indicate that four-year colleges experience declining per-student costs until 5,363 FTE students are enrolled, a number considerably larger than Russell and Reeves's 1,050 students.

One source of difference in the estimates of the least-cost institutional size is attributable to the methodology used in fitting the function to the data. Russell and Reeves, had they fitted a function to their data by solving for the parameters in a least-squares quadratic equation, would have concluded that minimum costs obtained in an institution of about 1,800 FTE students. However, this discrepancy does not bridge all the difference between their function and the general function.

A second source of difference in the two functions may be traced to the manner in which the functions were derived. Russell and Reeves included, in their sample, schools of different types that were each subject to a unique set of influences on their abilities to raise revenues. That is, the per-student expenditure represented by each of the sample points in Russell and Reeves's study implicitly contained a unique set of circumstances under which the operating revenue was raised. In our study deliberate care was taken to avoid this source of possible noncomparability by attempting to hold constant the ability to raise revenue. On the other hand, it can be argued that the attempt was unsuccessful in rendering homogeneous the conditions under which revenue is

1. John Dale Russell and Floyd W. Reeves, *Finance*, vol. 7 of *The Evaluation of Higher Institutions* (Chicago: University of Chicago Press, 1937), pp. 20–36.

raised. The assumption of homogeneity is based on the fact that the basic study groups were institutions charging the same tuition and fees, and going to the same governor and legislature for their operating subsidy. It may be argued that the differential conditions of raising revenue implicit in Russell and Reeves's study were stochastic in behavior, in which case one would expect no change in the parameters of the derived cost function if enough observations were made. One could easily accept the latter argument to some degree, and conclude that the difference in methods used to arrive at the two functions represents the major cause for the difference in results.

To find the major source of difference between Russell and Reeves's function and the general function, one must explain what happened between the early 1930s and 1967–68 to cause average-cost functions for the two periods with such major differences in the coefficients. (Of course, any difference in the level of the two functions would be largely due to rising prices of factors, especially teachers and other human factors.) It is not too difficult to see what occurred between the early 1930s and the present to stretch-out, so to speak, the long-run average-cost function for IHL. The clue is to recall the analysis from Chapter 3 which suggested that a crucial determinant for the range over which declining costs might be realized would be the level of threshold staffing, especially threshold staffing of the teaching faculty. Thus, if threshold staffing has changed radically in the past forty or so years, and the change has been such that the levels of threshold staffing have grown over time, it would be true that the average-cost function would decline over a wider range of school sizes measured in FTE students. Of course, this is exactly what has happened.

The explosion in knowledge in the past few decades is well known and needs no documentation here. The result for the problem at hand has been a general increase in the size of the threshold faculty, primarily because instruction in most disciplines has become more specialized, as former areas of speciality within disciplines have split off into separate departments, and as completely new fields have been introduced into the colleges and universities. Also contributing to what, in effect, amounts to a higher level of fixed costs for IHL has been the extension of more services to all members of the academic community, for example, student counseling by specialists and institutional research formally and constantly conducted.

Current trends seem to suggest a kind of hypothesis about a dynamic theory of average costs for IHL: barring another Dark Age, threshold staffing should continue to grow over time and widen the range of institutional sizes over which declining average costs may be realized. As to the rate at which this has proceeded, or will proceed, there would have to be an intensive investigation of heretofore "uncharted seas."

Implications of the Four-Year IHL Long-Run Cost Function for Contemporary Higher Education

This study has concentrated on the nature of long-run costs in four-year colleges, and it is not intended to dwell at length on any suggested implications of the nature of these costs. However, given the quantitative nature of the general function, two contemporary phenomena of American higher education deserve brief comment: (1) the financial difficulties of the private institutions and (2) the rationale for the modern public "multiversity." To aid in this discussion, Table 5.1 shows the distribution of universities and four-year teachers' and liberal arts colleges, by FTE students, in the fall of 1967.

It is generally agreed by interested observers today that private higher education is in real financial difficulty. The AAUP reports that "an air of crisis hangs over private institutions of higher

TABLE 5.1

ALL UNIVERSITIES AND FOUR-YEAR TEACHERS AND LIBERAL ARTS COLLEGES,
BY FTE STUDENTS, FALL, 1967

	Universities Public		Private	
FTE Students	Number	Percent	Number	Percent
Under 5,000	9	8.7	23	32.4
5,000–9,999	28	27.2	33	46.5
10,000–14,999	26	25.2	8	11.3
15,000–19,999	24	23.3	4	5.7
20,000–24,999	3	2.9	2	2.8
25,000 and over	13	12.6	1	1.4
	Four-Year Colleges			
Under 1,500	85	25.3	637	77.5
1,500–2,999	83	24.7	152	18.5
3,000–4,499	63	18.8	16	1.9
4,500–5,999	38	11.3	9	1.0
6,000–7,499	29	8.6	3	0.4
7,500–8,999	14	4.2	3	0.4
9,000–10,499	10	3.0	—	—
10,500 and over	14	4.2	2	0.2

SOURCE: Computed from Office of Education, *Opening Fall Enrollments, 1967*.

NOTE: The percent columns may not add to 100.0 because of rounding.

learning. . . . It is not difficult to compile an impressive list of private institutions which can make ends meet only by constant recourse to emergency measures."[2] However, the reasons for this financial crisis are not as often agreed upon as is the fact that a crisis does exist.

Although the ideas are not mutually exclusive, conventional wisdom attributes the financial plight of private IHL to (1) the growing differential in student fees at public as opposed to

2. "The Economic Status of the Profession," p. 183.

private IHL, while the differences in the nature of the product of each does not seem accurately to reflect differences in these student fees or (2) the more rapid increase in per-student costs at private IHL in recent years, as opposed to public institutions.

The first school of thought would go something like this: (1) in the past, especially before World War II, there was a rather clear distinction between the roles and products of private and public IHL, and the public generally accepted the differences in finances of the two as being consistent with the differences in function and product; (2) for sundry and complex reasons, the differences in functions and products of private and public IHL have narrowed in the post–World War II period; but (3) the finances of the two types of IHL have not undergone much change, and the result today is that private and public IHL provide similar products of similar quality, but the direct cost to the student for private higher education is a significant multiple of the cost for about the same thing provided by the public college or university. The result has been about what economic theory or intuition would suggest—that when two firms charge significantly different prices for a product that is little differentiated, customers turn increasingly to the firm charging the lower price. In 1955 about 52 percent of all college students were in public institutions; in 1967, this percentage had increased to 70.[3] In 1955 the mean monetary differential between tuition and required fees in private and public IHL was $299; by 1967 this differential had increased to $657 annually.[4] Thus, Cartter warns:

> If there is not a sharp change in pricing philosophy (and/or subsidizing philosophy) on the part of the state institutions, it seems likely that many private colleges and universities will be in serious

3. Bureau of the Census, *Statistical Abstract, 1968*.
4. Ibid.

difficulty. If public institutions were to narrow the price differential by markedly raising their tuition levels, and perhaps using most of the increased income to underwrite needy students, the private colleges (which are operating closer to full-cost pricing) would have a better chance to remain fiscally healthy.[5]

The alternative position often taken considers the high costs of the private schools, as compared to those of their public counterparts, to be the major source of the former's financial difficulties. The AAUP reports as follows:

> Current expenditures *per-student* in the nonpublic institutions (in 1965–66 dollars) rose from $1875 in 1955–56 to $3102 in 1965–66, an increase of about 65 per cent.
>
> To avoid any misunderstanding, let us be clear that the cost problem . . . also exists in public institutions, but in a less pronounced form. Presumably because of factors such as increased use of teaching assistants, faster growth in class sizes, and a slower rate of increase in outlays for organized research relative to enrollment, current expenditures in the public institutions have gone up less rapidly than they have in private colleges and universities.[6]

Of course the two positions are reconcilable. The private IHL, more than the public schools, are caught in a costs-income squeeze in real and current terms, and one can talk of either an excess of costs or a shortage of income. However, a strategic determinant of per-student costs is often excluded from the discussion, and this should be brought explicitly to the forefront. Put simply, the private IHL find their competitive position vis-à-vis the public institutions deteriorating partly because their growth has not allowed them to offset the increased costs of inflation, and to provide more and better services and academic programs, with savings through the realization of economies of scale. On the other hand, the public IHL have increased and

5. Allan M. Cartter, "The Economics of Higher Education," p. 162.
6. "Economic Status," pp. 183–184.

upgraded their programs and services in recent years, probably as much as private IHL; however, the additional costs of expanded activities have been canceled out, to some extent, by the positive realization of greater economies of scale.

Certainly, the analysis of Chapter 4 (see pp. 110–112) suggests there is no significant difference in either the student–all personnel or student-teacher ratios in public or private IHL of the same size. It may be suggested that the differences in real costs per student, between the public and private IHL, are largely attributable to one thing: *The private schools usually are simply too small to enjoy the economies of scale realized by the larger public institutions.*

A glance at Table 5.1 will serve to dramatize this contention. With an enrollment of about 5,363 FTE students allowing maximum economies of scale in four-year colleges, 96 percent of private liberal arts and teachers' colleges had less than 3,000 FTE students in fall, 1967. However, only one-half of the public four-year colleges fell in this "inefficient" range, with the remainder located in the low-cost range of 3,000 and upwards FTE students.

This study does not quantify a long-run cost function for the university. However, since universities typically have more academic programs, at more instructional levels, than do four-year colleges, it would be expected that universities would have falling per-student costs over a wider range of FTE students because of a larger threshold faculty. One can only make a semi-informed guess at this point, but it may be suggested that, given the distribution of students among the various programs and levels of instruction at the "typical" university, maximum economies of scale would come at between 9,000 and 10,000 FTE students. In fall, 1967, about 79 percent of all private universities had less than 10,000 FTE students, while only about 36 percent of all public universities were in this same category.

Thus, one must look to the small size of the private school for a major factor explaining its financial plight, especially since this plight is a *relative* one. It is not the intent here to disparage the small college or university—in fact, there will be more about this type of institution shortly. What should be made clear is that private schools must recognize that they are paying for their smallness relative to public institutions, and if smallness is a matter of choice, it must also be recognized that it results in a monetary and real cost passed on to students in the form of higher than would-be tuition and fees, or to employees in the form of lower than would-be wages. But it may be that both students and employees are willing to bear this cost.

Although the majority of public four-year colleges and universities seem to be in an enrollment range that allows a substantial realization of internal economies of scale, a good many of them are far beyond the enrollment figure necessary for minimum per-student costs. The large school raises a question that may be equal in importance to the one concerning the wisdom of having small, high-cost, schools. Unfortunately for the scientist, the question does not lend itself readily to the application of objective analysis.

It may be noted at the outset that many economists reject any notion that, as regards the firm, "bigness" and "goodness" are synonymous for all degrees of bigness. It would be fair to say, for example, that most economists and other social scientists find no real virtue in the gigantic American corporations whose size is far in excess of that necessary to realize maximum economies of scale. Professor Stigler opines: "I personally believe that future study will confirm the traditional belief that big businesses, for all their resources, cannot rival the infinite resource and cold scrutiny of many independent and competing companies."[7]

7. George J. Stigler, "The Case Against Big Business," in *Monopoly Power and Economic Performance*, ed. Edwin Mansfield (New York: Norton), p. 9.

Professor Kaysen, speaking about the effect of the large corporations, writes that "a few large corporations exert significant power . . . over the whole of society with respect to many choices, and over large segments of it with respect to others."[8] Professor Bain typifies the concern over the gigantic firm, and suggests that "so far as [public] policy affects private business enterprise, one important goal is often put forward: *the prohibition of undue size on the part of the business enterprises*, and the preservation of a large population of relatively small firms" (emphasis added).[9]

However, a consideration of the gigantic "firm" in higher education would involve examining the relationship between the size of the institution and the legitimate goals of higher education. It appears that there are at least two reasons why it is unwise for IHL to grow much past the size necessary to realize minimum per-student costs.

First, there seems to be an adverse effect on students by virtue of attendance at gigantic, as contrasted to small or moderately sized, schools. One investigator, Roberta D. Brown, who studied the environmental influence of large versus small schools, writes the following:

> To determine whether the student was having a successful college experience, the study examined three criteria: freshman grade point average, retention over a four-semester period, and participation in extracurricular activities. . . .
>
> Examination . . . would indicate that the data seem to favor the small private college on all three criteria. Students in [the small college] had higher grade point averages, a higher retention rate, and participation to a greater extent in extracurricular activities.[10]

8. Carl Kaysen, "The Corporation: How Much Power? What Scope?" *The Corporation in Modern Society*, ed. Edward Mason (Cambridge, Mass.: Harvard University Press), p. 85.

9. Joe S. Bain, *Industrial Organization*, 2d ed. (John Wiley & Sons, 1968), p. 499.

10. Roberta D. Brown, "Student Characteristics and Institutional Impact of the Large Publicly Controlled vs. the Small Private Institution," *College and University* 42, no. 3 (Spring 1967): 331.

With regard to student demonstrations and their relationship to the institutional environment, another investigator, Richard E. Peterson, found that

> the factor of size, the increasingly mass nature of much of American higher education with the presumed attendant alienation and reduced sense of self, is the institutional characteristic that has perhaps been most widely pointed to by journalists and other observers in attempting to rationalize the new student unrest.[11]

The bureaucracy and regimentation that seem necessary in a school of 15,000; 20,000; 30,000; or 40,000 students may be incompatible with what should be a personal educational experience. If there is no hard, cold economic advantage to a university of 20,000 students, as opposed to two schools of 10,000 students, there must be other reasons explaining the existence of the gigantic institution. In fact, there appear to be *no reasonable* noneconomic justifications for the existence of "multiversities" and on balance the noneconomic effect of the gigantic institution seems debilitating to both students and faculty.

Second, the gigantic IHL (with rare exceptions) must draw students from a large area, many of them consequently living at school. This is an inefficient use of society's resources because it results in a duplication of housing, a commodity already in too short supply in the United States. That is, for each student living on campus, there likely is adequate, unused housing at his parents' home. However, society ends up providing duplicate facilities if the college student does not live at home, and this duplication is either in terms of a proliferation of dormitories or private, college-town housing. The implication is not that, on balance, total social costs of higher education would be lower if

11. Richard E. Peterson, *The Scope of Organized Student Protest in 1964–65* (Princeton, N.J.: Educational Testing Service, 1966), p. 23.

all students were able to live at home while attending college. It is to hold, however, that any area which is large enough to support either a university or four-year college, in terms of an efficient number of FTE students, should have such an institution in preference to one large state university drawing its students from urban areas throughout the state. It may be noted that some states are now acting on this principle.

In closing, it is appropriate to comment on some of the reasons why some IHL tend to grow well past the smallest size necessary for minimum per-student costs. First, few people have any idea where the least-cost size might be; perhaps the present study will help explain how to arrive at this point. Second, it seems as if the notion has evolved in this country that the decision making, not just the administration, in higher education should rest with the academic community. There really has not been much discussion outside the public IHL concerning the role and direction that public higher education ought to take. Such discussions have not been initiated by a public which perhaps feels that the subject is too esoteric; on the other hand, the academic community in public IHL have not been disposed voluntarily to share their power over higher education policy. Third, in many states those who are concerned about the quality of the educational process have concluded that public subsidy for new physical facilities will be forthcoming only when existing structures are inadequate in terms of physical capacity, and that inadequacy in a functional sense can only be remedied by outgrowing the old facilities. Fourth, to the extent that the effects of institutional growth have been considered, there seems to be a consensus that per-student costs become constant at quite a low level of total enrollments, and that any deleterious effects of large schools must be nonexistent or, at worst, miniscule. Finally, and perhaps most crucially, higher education decision makers have viewed the physical plant with awe, and have evaluated plant requirements for new institutions in terms of the initial and absolute costs alone, and not as an outlay to be depreciated over many students and some considerable period of time. The last point requires more elaboration.

It is rather easy to argue that about 97–99 percent of the total per-student costs of higher education are noncapital costs, and that decisions on the establishment of new institutions should only be concerned with the likelihood of the new institution quickly reaching an FTE student level that allows maximum economies of scale. However, the capital markets for IHL have some serious defects. Coombs writes:

> Where rising demand for a product would guarantee that most industries could get additional real capital, institutions of higher learning find themselves in an opposite situation. Tradition and/or law often prevents bond financing and gifts must often be dependent upon the fortuitous death of a wealthy donor. Some public institutions also find their access to funds for capital purposes limited by the general squeeze on government revenues.[12]

Thus, there is a kind of dichotomy. On the one hand, there are a number of private IHL too small to realize maximum economies of scale and in serious financial straits at least partly for this reason. On the other hand, one finds the public schools in rather sound financial health, partly because they are realizing maximum economies of scale, subsidizing and upgrading graduate and professional programs from a surplus realized on undergraduate programs, but growing to a size that threatens the real substance of what a higher education should be. The obvious answer is to channel additional students into the smaller schools, public or private, bringing them to an efficient size and, perhaps, pursuing positive policies to reduce gradually the size of the "multiversities." The wisdom of such a plan seems to be sound

12. Philip H. Coombs, "An Economist's Overview," pp. 21–22.

and obvious. The means to do it are really in the hands of the several state legislatures. Like many needed institutional reforms in America, this one will not come soon.

Summary

Although there is agreement with Russell and Reeves concerning the general shape of a long-run cost function for IHL, there is some disagreement on the specific shape of such a function. Specifically, Russell and Reeves would establish the FTE student level, allowing minimum per-student costs, at about 1,050 students, while the general function developed in Chapter 4 would put this least-cost enrollment at 5,363 FTE students.

A minor source of difference is found in the fact that Russell and Reeves fitted their function by observation, while a function fitted by least-squares would have established the least-cost enrollment at about 1,800 FTE students. Also, Russell and Reeves's sample included schools which likely were raising revenue under diverse conditions, while the general function attempted to hold constant these influences on revenue. However, neither of these facts account for the majority of the difference between 1,050 and 5,363 students.

The general function differed from Russell and Reeves's in a technical sense in that the coefficients for the independent variable had major disparities. The reason is not too difficult to find if the analysis of Chapter 3 is recalled. There it was noted that a critical determinant for the shape of the average-cost function would be the level of threshold staffing, especially the level of the threshold teaching staff.

It appears that between the early 1930s (the period for which Russell and Reeves derived their function) and 1967–68 there has been a general increase in the level of threshold staffing in IHL, and it has resulted in a wider range of institutional sizes in which declining per-student costs may be realized. The notion would certainly have validity if it is accepted that the level of threshold staffing of the institution is a function of the breadth and depth of services provided to all members of the academic community. It is valid of course, because the knowledge explosion in recent times has had the effect of requiring a larger threshold teaching staff. Also contributing in the same fashion has been a tendency to increase the provision of nominally nonacademic services.

Although it is not the intention to explore fully here the implications of the general function for contemporary IHL, two well-known problems do seem to be related closely to this function. The first is the current financial crisis of the private IHL; the second is the rationale for the gigantic "multiversity," which is largely a phenomenon of the public sector.

There is generally wide agreement that private IHL are in grave financial difficulties, because their product is not much differentiated from that of the public schools, while there is a considerable and growing spread in tuition and other academic fees charged by each type of IHL. However, the growing differential has been related to a growing spread in cost per student between the two types of institutions. It has not been explicitly recognized that one reason costs in private IHL have been growing faster than in public IHL is that the latter have increased in size and enjoyed some cost savings from realization of economies of scale. On the other hand, almost all private four-year colleges are still in the highly inefficient FTE student ranges. Thus, a major explanation for the widening cost spread between private and public IHL is that as both have expanded the depth and breadth of programs and services, the public institutions have been able to offset some of the additional costs by growing in size and realizing economies of scale—the private schools have not done this.

The four-year IHL long-run cost function was not intended to be applied directly to the universities, but a semiinformed guess would establish the minimum cost point in a "typical" university at 9,000 to 10,000 FTE students. Certainly, many public "multiversities" have grown well past this point, and it must be recognized there are noneconomic effects of size in higher education; on balance these effects are probably detrimental as the institution keeps growing larger. Also, total social costs of higher education are increased by the "multiversity" because growth past the least-cost point brings no more operational economies of scale, but does require more students to live away from home.

Finally, it must be recognized that the "multiversity" has been a product of (1) forces with a vested interest in such an institution and (2) public officials unable to face the short-run, initial capital outlays required for the establishment of new institutions when existing institutions have grown to an economical size. The existing higher education scene, with most schools either much smaller or much larger than necessary to realize minimum per-student costs, certainly makes little sense, economically or in other ways. However, this is by no means the most pressing issue that society is currently facing, and there seems little prospect of change.

Appendix A

Peripheral Activities of
Institutions of Higher Learning

This appendix presents a theoretical discussion of the determinants of some activities of colleges and universities which are
not (1) common to all schools or (2) primarily intended to be an
integral part of the resident instruction program. The latter
characterization may be debated, especially in the case of
organized research. But whether or not any activity discussed in
this appendix is, indeed, an integral part of the resident instruction program makes little difference for the microeconomic
analysis of the activity. The analysis here will proceed in the same
manner as in Chapter 3; that is, a combination of factual statistical
data and logical inference is used to develop a theory concerning
the influences on costs in the several activities.

Organized Research and Other Sponsored Programs

The activity entitled other sponsored programs is characterized by funding from a source other than the school itself, and
much of the research conducted by IHL is partially or wholly
funded by entities outside the academic community. It would be
expected that outside entities desire the research activity to be
performed in certain areas of academic interest. This is not to
suggest that all research funds, from sources other than the
schools' normal revenues, are highly restricted. But it does
suggest that IHL do not have the same autonomy in the use of
these research funds as they do in the disposition of their general
revenues.

There is much that motivates the federal government or, say, General Motors to sponsor research or institutes at one school but not another. The most important factor seems to be the apparent ability of personnel at the various institutions successfully and adequately to discharge research responsibilities. Thus, it may be noted that "nationwide Federal [research and development] support to universities and colleges tends to be concentrated in a few institutions."[1] And further, "A closer examination reveals that Federal funds to seven universities are largely responsible [for the fact that 37 percent of the total federal research and development support went to the three states of New York, California, and Massachusetts]: in New York, both Columbia and Cornell Universities; in California, the University of California, at Los Angeles and Berkeley, and Stanford University; in Massachusetts, the Massachusetts Institute of Technology and Harvard."[2]

As was mentioned above, some IHL devote general revenues to formal research activity, often as a matter of course, and such research appears to have a little different motivation than that financed by federal or private support. In the first place it is obvious that research is a necessary function of higher education, and most schools accept the idea, some by regularly devoting general funds to this end. For the public institutions, James L. Miller notes that some state legislatures, as a matter of course, make regular allowance for expenditures on organized research by their institutions, and the amount so budgeted is often arrived at by calculating some percentage of another budget activity (for example, 5 percent of instruction and departmental research).[3] And it appears that some private schools have made a policy

1. National Science Foundation, *Geographic Distribution of Federal Funds for Research and Development: Fiscal Year 1965*, p. 21.

2. Ibid.

3. James L. Miller, *State Budgeting: for Higher Education* (Ann Arbor, Mich.: University of Michigan Institute of Public Administration, 1964), chapter 5.

decision to devote some portion of their total educational and general budget to organized research.

Thus, the determinants of the level of separately budgeted research at a given school would be varied, and it would be difficult to quantify each of these determinants. To the extent that funds are devoted to formal research in some ratio to other educational and general activities, it could be said that the levels of these latter activities (and their determinants) will, in turn, influence the level of IHL-performed formal research. However, given the heavy participation today of the federal government in the funding of research activity, one would be inclined to conclude that the majority of all research conducted at IHL is determined by such subjective criteria as the supposed quality of the faculty at the various schools.

One other thing that may be noted about formal research in IHL is that "a good deal of research in universities still does not appear cost-wise in the accounting category 'organized research' [and consequently] as an item of university expenditure is not necessarily the entire cost of the research work done by a university."[4] It would be difficult to identify the portion of instruction and departmental research actually devoted to research, but it might be suggested that whatever is so spent serves as a kind of alternative source of support for faculty unable to get research support elsewhere, and such "covert" support should not exhibit any systematic tendencies among various schools.

The research conducted at IHL is *not* directly attributable to phenomena subject to objective quantification, although this generalization is surely susceptible to exceptions, some of which were noted above. It is sufficient to note here that research

---

4. John D. Millett, *The Staff Report of the Commission on Financing Higher Education: Financing Higher Education in the United States* (New York: Columbia University Press, 1952), p. 126.

activity is likely to be more a function of the type of school (for example, university, four-year college, junior college), than a function of the scale of operations at a particular school. There is no reason to suppose research activity in IHL is a direct function of the size of the institution.

Extension and Public Service

The activities grouped under extension and public service are, like research, not subject to the same influences that work upon the more direct educational functions. IHL have long recognized their responsibilities to be of service to the general public and students other than those in residence. The public IHL dominate these activities, employing about 90 percent of all professional personnel assigned to extension and public service in recent years.[5] Even this statistic overstates the role of private IHL in extension because one private school, Cornell University, has the land-grant college obligations in its state, and dominates total private IHL extension and public service.

Public institutions find that their extension and public service programs, which provide contact with nonstudents, are mutually beneficial to both. Correspondence and other instructional programs, when offered, incur costs in some proportion to (1) enrollments and (2) the scope of offerings. The various "short courses" conducted by the public universities give rise to total expenditures that are likely more closely correlated with the number of courses than with the total number of attendees. However, within the broad category of extension and public service, the dominant area, accounting for upward of three-fourths of total extension and public service expenditures in recent years, is agriculture.[6]

5. U.S. Dept. of HEW, Office of Education, *Faculty and Other Professional Staff in Institutions of Higher Learning, 1963–64* (Washington, D.C.: GPO).
6. *Budget Studies.*

The major extension and public service expenditures related to agriculture are devoted to the Agricultural Extension Service, experiment stations, and other direct services to agriculture. Millett has written the following:

> Governmental action singled out the farm group in our society as especially in need of a particular kind of adult and part-time educational service. . . . The level of [extension and public service] expenditure reflects the political influences which are brought to bear upon this part of the educational budget.[7]

Also, in schools without land-grant college responsibilities, it is the practice of some legislatures to allocate to extension and public service an amount equal to a percentage of some or all of the educational and general budgets of their institutions.[8]

In sum, extension and public service costs are largely influenced by subjective phenomena, much as is the case with research. Some of these activities (such as correspondence study) would likely show a substantial correlation between an objective measure (students) and costs, but the majority of total extension and public service expenditures are attributable to agricultural programs at the land-grant colleges, the levels of which are probably a function of specific agricultural conditions and the political power of the farm sector.

Summary

Organized research and other sponsored programs, two standard accounting activities in higher education, seem to be little influenced by anything easily subject to quantitative description. Rather, the apparent abilities of an institution's staff seem to be the prime determinant of the level of research

7. Millett, *Staff Report*, p. 121.
8. Miller, *State Budgeting*, chapter 5.

financed from outside the school and of the level of the institution's total research expenditures.

Likewise, extension and public service expenditures are mainly influenced by things other than what would be called characteristics of the institution. Especially the expenditures on agricultural programs, which dominate total extension and public service expenditures, are and continue to be the product of a political decision which has singled out the agribusiness industry for special assistance.

Appendix B

The Statistical Derivation of the Four-Year IHL Long-Run Cost Function

This appendix describes in detail the methodology used in arriving at the empirical relationship between costs and students presented in Chapter 4. The description will comprise three parts: (1) the considerations that were necessary when choosing the IHL that composed the statistical sample will be discussed; (2) the statistical methods used to compute the cost functions for each element in the general function will be explained and illustrated; and (3) aggregation of the four-year IHL long-run cost function, from the elements that emerge from item 2, above, will be presented.

IHL Composition of the Study

A cross-section approach to estimating a long-run cost function basically "photographs" a number of producing entities at a point in time, and then attempts to use the photograph to characterize the behavior of a single producing entity in the long run with only the price of inputs and technology fixed. Thus, one assumes that the actual behavior of *various* producing entities represents a close approximation to the expected behavior of *one* producer. The key to the cross-section approach is that, unlike time series data, the former freezes money prices and technology.

There are, however, some difficulties inherent when making this assumption, all related to one likelihood: when the photograph was taken, all the sample or universe points might not have been homogeneous in that, had all been producing at exactly the same scale, their costs would have differed. A short discussion of some specific phenomena that can give rise to heterogeneity, and how it may apply to higher education, will serve to explain the composition of this empirical study.

First, the firms (using this term to characterize any entity converting resources into a product or service) may not be producing identical products to an extent that significantly affects costs. If one were reconciling the differences in per-unit costs realized in a plant producing Rolls Royces, as opposed to Volkswagens, the scale of operation of the two plants would not logically be the first thing explored. Likewise, the output of various and sundry IHL differs a great deal in terms of the real cost per unit. Some would call this a difference in quality; the interest here is only in the fact that differences in real inputs per units of output exist—the results of this variation are not the subject of this study. There is presently no way to measure the quality of the product that results from the operations of a given teacher, department, college, or university; thus, the study concentrates on IHL that seem to have some uniformity in the application of resources per unit of output, given the scale of output. It seems that this leads the analysis from private IHL to the public schools.

One would expect private IHL to vary greatly in their abilities to secure resources. For one thing the private IHL exhibit much greater diversity in their level of student fees than do a group of similar, state-controlled IHL within a given state. The private IHL secure their budget subsidy from a multitude of private and public benefactors, and the ability of specific private IHL to gain their subsidy differs greatly. On the other hand, the public four-year schools in many states are increasingly subject to a formula approach for making operating appropriations from state funds, and such an approach is rather uniform if nothing else.[1] In the last analysis, the major determinant of the level of a school's expenditures is the revenue available; one would expect more uniformity in the ability to raise operating revenue among a group of public institutions, subject to the same legislature, same governor, same coordinating council, and often the same governing board, than would be the case for any group of private IHL. This uniformity was the major consideration in choosing, as the basic study group, all state-controlled four-year colleges within a state.

A second source of variation in costs due to differences in the nature of the product, when applied to higher education, involves the objective mix of the levels and types of instructional offerings. Ideally, one would study institutions with an identical mix of workload among the various teaching departments and levels of instruction. The present study utilizes the federal government's designation of four-year public colleges. It is certainly not assumed that each four-year public college in each state has identical distributions of students among lower-division, upper-division, and graduate study, or among the various disciplines; however, such measures as the types of degrees offered, or the ratio of FTE graduate to undergraduate students, did not often appear to be significantly different in the group of institutions used here. However, again it is emphasized that the federal government's designations were used except for some exceptions to be noted later.

The third source of divergence in costs among firms, given the level of output, is the relationship between (1) actual short-run level of utilization of physical plant and (2) the most efficient level. Professor Bain warns that the "long-run average cost

1. See Miller, *State Budgeting*, chapters 4–6.

curve . . . assumes that the scale of the firm and the rate of use of any plant factors are coordinated and simultaneously adjusted *so as to produce any chosen output at the lowest possible cost*'' (emphasis added).[2] Applied to IHL, the most desirable situation for cross-section studies would be for all schools to utilize their physical plants and other inputs in the least-cost combination. In lieu of this perfect state, random departures from least-cost short-run combinations should leave unaffected the level and shape of any derived function. There appears to be no uniform way to determine whether there are systematic tendencies among large, small, rural, urban, public, or private IHL to be overbuilt, or to be subject to other sources of short-run inefficiencies. However, there is no evidence of systematic tendencies among any of the aforementioned types of IHL, and an assumption implicit in this study is that such tendencies are random.

Finally, if the money prices for similar inputs differ greatly among the elements of a cross section, and they go unadjusted, the resulting function will not be solely a reflection of different factor combinations per unit of output at various scale levels. Conceivably, there are many influences which could result in two different IHL paying different money prices for the same factor of production. And, because of the labor-intensity of higher education, labor is the factor of most concern. It was suggested above (see pp. 55–57) that the region of the country in which a school is located will have a significant influence on its money costs for both professional and nonprofessional personnel. But within a region there may well be substantial variations among IHL in their money costs for personnel, and it would be desirable, if possible, to reduce these variations. Table B.1 shows computed ratios for each of the thirteen states studied, such ratios expressing the relationship between highest and lowest institutional average salary for full-time faculty; the computation for public schools

2. Bain, *Price Theory*, p. 111.

TABLE B.1

RATIO, HIGHEST TO LOWEST AVERAGE INSTITUTIONAL FULL-TIME
FACULTY SALARY, PUBLIC AND PRIVATE: SUBJECT STATES, 1967–68

State Number	Public IHL	Private IHL
1[a]	1.1	2.2
2	1.4	1.3
3	1.1	1.9
4	1.2	1.3
5	—	1.3
6	1.0	1.7
7	1.1	1.5
8	1.2	1.3
9	1.1	1.4
10	1.2	1.8
11	1.0	1.5
12	1.2	1.3
13	1.0	1.4
All	1.5	2.7

SOURCE: "The Economic Status of the Profession."

[a] 1966–67 data.

utilizes the IHL from this study, while the private IHL ratio for
each state applies to all their four-year colleges, with the exception that only schools making their salary data available could
be used.

In only one state (number 2) of the twelve for which data were
available did the ratio for public IHL exceed that for private
schools, and the margin was but 1.38 to 1.29. If one wishes to
minimize factor price differentials for the major class of labor by
studying institutions within one geographical area, public four-
year colleges within an individual state are far more homogeneous than private schools within one state.

The considerations most likely to invalidate a cross-section
study's conclusions could be summarized as

1. A difference in the nature of the product significant enough to affect substantially per-unit costs at similar output levels
2. A significant difference in the mix of products, if there is an element of multiproduct operation involved
3. Differences in the money prices of inputs

Applied to higher education, it appears that the public four-year colleges within a particular state represent a study group superior to any subjective selection of private schools because they (1) are likely to be subject to more uniform and objective processes for determining the operating subsidy that all institutions require; (2) do not appear to differ very much from private IHL in the mixture of efforts among instructional levels or broad disciplines; and (3) demonstrate more homogeneity than do their private counterparts, in the money prices paid for the quantitatively most important input.

Two other matters require explanation to conclude this section on the composition of the study. First, the manner of determining the states included and the implications flowing therefrom will be discussed. Second, the instances of exclusion of some institutions within a given state will be outlined.

It was decided, considering the statistical methods to be used, that not all states could be included in the study. Specifically, the following criteria were used to determine the states to be studied:

1. At least four four-year colleges (not universities) in one state
2. A total range of 3,000 FTE students at minimum
3. No more than one-fifth of the total four-year colleges in the state eliminated for reasons discussed below

These criteria were motivated by a desire to have a somewhat wide dispersion about the mean institutional size within each state and to begin the study where other investigators had left off.

There were also five reasons to exclude individual IHL:

1. Operations begun after fall, 1966 (in effect, a school had to be at least two years old at the conclusion of 1967–68)
2. FTE enrollment of less than 500 in fall, 1967
3. Operation of campuses in more than one city
4. A student body composed of more than 95 percent of one sex
5. Evidence from the state that an institution was budgeted in 1967–68 as either a university or two-year college

In the solicitation of data, comprehensive financial information was received on all public IHL in twenty-six states; of the remainder, it appeared that, based upon the criteria established above, ten states could have been used had their data been obtained. The other fourteen states would not have been used, even if data had been obtained, because each had three or less public schools. Of the twenty-six states for which comprehensive data were obtained, thirteen were not used for the following reasons:

1. Eight states either had three or less four-year colleges, or the elimination of single schools brought their total to this cutoff point.
2. Four states had at least four eligible institutions, but not an adequate size distribution.
3. One state had more than one-fifth of its institutions eliminated on the basis of criteria for excluding individual institutions.

The thirteen states that were used contained 131 public four-year IHL, or about 40 percent of the national total of this type of institution. Eight institutions from these 131 were eliminated on the basis of criteria listed above: 3 were multicity operations, 1 had less than 500 students, and the rest appeared to have been budgeted as either junior colleges or universities. Since the study contained four of the five largest states in terms of enrollments in public four-year institutions, it represented about 60 percent of all students in public four-year colleges in fall, 1967.

There appears to be no reason to conclude that the responses to requests for data were anything but random; thus, it is assumed (1) the states included in the study represent a non-biased sample of eligible states; (2) the results are applicable to all public four-year IHL; and (3) to the extent that private IHL are similar to public schools, as discussed in Chapter 4, above, the results also apply to all private four-year IHL.

Computation of the Intermediate Long-Run Cost Functions

Once the composition of the sample was determined, the computation of intermediate cost functions was rather mechanical. However, the two-step process will be described in detail.

The initial step in computing the intermediate functions for each state involved establishing the level of FTE students, and computing an adjusted measure of educational and general expenditures per student. In some instances the suppliers of financial data also provided information on their FTE enrollments; when they did, their statistic was used. Although not absolutely uniform, the FTE student has generally come to be defined as either thirty undergraduate, or twenty-four graduate, semester hours, with appropriate conversions made for schools on a quarter system. The FTE student has become a standard unit of higher educational workload measurement as part-time attendance has become more common, especially in the urban public school.

When FTE data were not supplied by the state, it was necessary to estimate a similar measure. For their estimates of FTE academic students, the Department of Health, Education and Welfare totals all full-time students and one-third of the part-time students. For this study more success was obtained with a modification to one-half of total part-time students, perhaps because many administrative functions are probably more related to head counts than to FTE students. In fact, the whole student services function could be described in this fashion. At any rate one of two measures of institutional size was used in this study, (1) FTE student measures supplied by the state or (2) all full-time students, graduate and undergraduate, plus one-half of all part-time students.

Once the number of FTE students was identified for each institution in the state, total per-student adjusted educational and general expenditures were computed. As described in Chapter 4, this computation is equal to total noncapital educational and general expenditures, minus the totals for organized research, extension and public service, and other sponsored programs, divided by FTE students. It is hereafter called average cost per student.

One final word of explanation is in order before moving to the calculus, and it concerns the computation of cost per student when expenditures data are for a fiscal (not academic) year, and the FTE student measure is for fall students only. Collegiate accounting typically establishes an expenditure account for summer sessions, and debits this with teaching salary expense only, in effect assuming that teaching salaries are the only expense incurred during summer sessions. On a marginal cost basis, this is probably rational because most of the remaining educational and general costs (general and academic administration and operation and maintenance of the plant, for example) are calendar year functions. However, this type of summer sessions accounting does result in a statistical allocation of the afore-mentioned calendar year functions to academic year students only. If instructional salary costs per credit hour in summer approximate those of regular sessions, a conversion of summer session credit-hours produced to an FTE student basis—using the thirty to twenty-four hour basis and the division of fiscal year costs by regular and summer sessions FTE students—results in all costs being spread over all terms.

In this study there was always present one of three cases:

1. Academic-year expenditures were supplied with academic-year FTE students.
2. Fiscal-year expenditures were supplied with fiscal-year FTE students.
3. Financial data alone were supplied, with specification as to whether fiscal or academic year, and the estimate of FTE students was made accordingly.

In such a manner there was consistency in computations within a state, which was the most important consideration.

Once cost per student was computed, a least-squares function was fitted to the data for each state using

$$y' = a + bx \qquad (1)$$

and

$$y' = a + bx + cx^2 \qquad (2)$$

where y' is predicted per-student cost; x is the institution size measured in FTE students; and a, b, and c are constants determining the shape and position of the function. The solutions from (2) were presented in Table 4.2. In Table B.2 columns 2 and 3 contain the coefficients and indices of determination for each state's data fitted by (1) and (2) respectively, and column 4 lists the sign of the slope coefficient for computations using (1).

At this juncture it is appropriate to discuss the intermediate cost functions in relation to tests of significance. Each of the thirteen intermediate functions represents universe, not sample, data. That is, within each of the thirteen states, no sampling was done; thus, tests of significance estimating the probability of the constants assuming some value owing to sampling vagaries are

TABLE B.2

INDICES AND COEFFICIENTS OF DETERMINATION, PARABOLIC AND LINEAR
FUNCTIONS, AND SIGN OF SLOPE COEFFICIENT FOR LINEAR FUNCTION

State Number	Parabolic	Linear	Sign, Linear Slope Coefficient
1	.8233	.6276	Negative
2	.6006	.4436	Positive
3	.5005	.4420	Negative
4	.6937	.4181	Negative
5	.9596	.4569	Negative
6	.9054	.7602	Negative
7	.4283	.2633	Negative
8	.7858	.6202	Negative
9	.9294	.0645	Negative
10	.5668	.4134	Negative
11	.5593	.5530	Positive
12	.4490	.4428	Negative
13	.6054	.1420	Negative

SOURCE: Computed from questionnaire data.

inappropriate. For example, if the data in each of the thirteen states had been sample data selected from a larger universe, it would be appropriate to test the significance of the difference between the index and coefficient of determination as listed in Table B.2. It would involve computing a variable F, which would be the difference in explained variation between the two statistics, adjusted for unexplained variance and degrees of freedom, and then testing a hypothesis concerning the significance of the explained variance. But when one has derived the universe index and coefficient of determination, a test of significance is meaningless. Of course, each state is considered a universe because there is a unique combination of influences, both in number and degree, working on the public IHL in each state.

Thus, as Table B.2 shows, in none of the states did a linear function seem more appropriate than a parabola for describing the relationship between institution size and per-student costs. It appears that the parabolic function best describes the long-run average-cost function for four-year schools. And as was shown in Table 4.2, a parabola convex to the abscissa, when the abscissa is in terms of institutional size, is obviously the appropriate slope of the parabola. The expectations and the empirical evidence both seem to support this conclusion.

Development of the Four-Year IHL Long-Run Cost Function

An objective of this study was to attempt to quantify what seems to be a consensus among those making decisions concerning the allocation of resources to IHL. It was done by using the intermediate cost functions to answer the following question: Given the evidence provided by these intermediate functions, what function would one expect to find if the consensus of IHL "technology" were known to all decision makers, and if the *only* influence on per-student costs from one four-year college to the next were the scale of operations? That is, the intermediate functions were used to compute a general function to be called the four-year IHL long-run cost function.

It was explained in Chapter 4 why the ordinate intercept is of no particular interest; it remains to explain the derivation of b and c in the general function. Repeated from Chapter 4, the four-year IHL long-run cost function was calculated over the range of 500 to 10,000 FTE students to be

$$y' = a - 0.244x + 0.00002275x^2 \tag{3}$$

Figure B.1 is a scatter diagram showing the thirteen sets of computed values for b and the indices of determination. A linear function fitted to these data, if the explained variance is significant, could be used to estimate b when r^2 was unity. The ability of the regression function to explain the variance in b rests on an assumption that the two variables are not related by definition. This is, indeed, the case; the model is not designed in such a way as to require that b and r^2 be related in any manner. But a relationship may exist that has meaning; it appears to be the case, and that b and r^2 should have a strong relationship because the net effect of the sum of all influences on per-student costs, other than the size of the institution, is to *equalize* per-student expenditures (through equalizing per-student appropriations), regardless of the size of the institution.

A linear function fitted to Figure B.1 cleared to

$$y' = 0.0762 - 0.32x \qquad (4)$$

where y' is the expected value of b when the index of determination assumes some value in the domain (x). The coefficient of correlation for (4) was .7552. And, since the data in Figure B.1 do not represent a universe (which would be the set of all possible states), tests of significance for the sample correlation are appropriate.

For linear correlation, the most common test of significance involves testing a hypothesis that there is *no* correlation in the universe data, given the size of the sample and the sample correlation coefficient. The student's t distribution is used in small sample problems in loco the standard error of estimate and the normal distribution.

For the data in Figure B.1, the t value was 3.845; an 0.005 significance level for eleven degrees of freedom is 3.4966. Thus, one would get sample data as in Figure B.1, from a universe that actually had zero correlation between the two variables b and r^2, less than five times in every thousand random samples of thirteen.

Setting x equal to 1.0 in (4), y' is -0.244 to three significant digits, which is the estimate of b for the general function. The

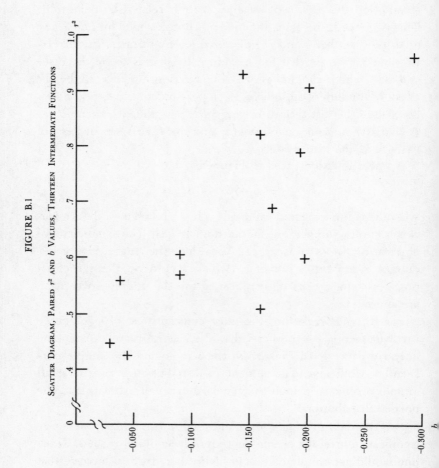

FIGURE B.1

SCATTER DIAGRAM, PAIRED r^2 AND b VALUES, THIRTEEN INTERMEDIATE FUNCTIONS

relationship between b and c in a parabola will determine, among other things, the position of the vertical axis of symmetry. This is of much interest because the vertical axis of symmetry will cross the abscissa at the point where the dependent variable is minimum. In other words the vertical axis of symmetry locates the *minimum-sized school necessary to realize all economies of scale*.

If there existed a perfect consensus among decision makers in all thirteen subject states concerning the quantitative nature of the long-run average-cost function, a scatter diagram plotting the combinations of b and c in the xy plane would result in a single point in quadrant II; that is, a single combination of b and c would be plotted thirteen times. As the real world departs from this perfect consensus, the geometric relationship portraying the paired values of b and c assumes two different dimensions. First, if the differences in the intermediate functions lie in the steepness of the sides of the parabola, with no difference in the vertical axis of symmetry, the plotted pairs of b and c values would fall exactly on a straight line with (1) a slope equal to one-half the reciprocal of the abscissa intercept of the vertical axis of symmetry and (2) an intercept at the origin. Second, as the real-world consensus differed somewhat on the location of the vertical axis of symmetry (or the minimum size of school necessary to realize all economies of scale), the plotted values for b and c would depart from the aforementioned straight line. Thus, if there is a consensus indicated by the thirteen intermediate functions, it should be shown by a tendency for plotted b and c pairs to fall on a straight line in quadrant II, and for the line to compress to a single point. Of course the slope of this line could then be manipulated to yield the x coordinate of the vertex of the general function.

As Figure B.2 (the plotted values of b and c for the intermediate functions) illustrates, the real-world consensus is not perfect among decision makers who, in effect, determine the

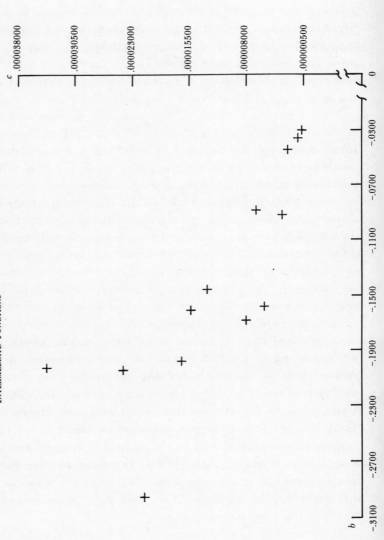

FIGURE B.2

SCATTER DIAGRAM, PAIRED b AND c VALUES, THIRTEEN
INTERMEDIATE FUNCTIONS

shape of the long-run average-cost curve for public four-year IHL in their respective states. This should not be surprising. However, a substantial consensus is indicated by just a visual examination of Figure B.2.

A least-squares regression function was fitted to the data in Figure B.2 and yielded

$$y' = 0.0000003066 - 0.0001058x \qquad (5)$$

with a coefficient of correlation of .7978. Thus, the departure of the real-world consensus from perfection was in terms of both the steepness of the function and the location of the vertical axis of symmetry. Of course here the primary interest is in the consensus on the location of the vertical axis of symmetry because the value of b for the general function has already been determined. If (5) fits the data closely, it may be assumed that a strong consensus exists concerning the location of the vertical axis of symmetry; and, with the value of b already determined, the value of c for the general function may be obtained by substituting -0.244 for x in (5) and evaluating.

Again the student's t distribution was used to test a hypothesis that the sample data in Figure B.2 came from a universe with zero correlation between c and b. A t value of about 4.4 was obtained, well outside the 3.4966 which is the 0.005 significance level with eleven degrees of freedom. It is, therefore, highly likely that the universe correlation is other than zero.

By setting x equal to -0.244 in (5) and evaluating, the value of 0.00002275 is obtained. This is the estimate of c for the general function.

Summary

The three steps leading to derivation of the four-year IHL long-run cost function were (1) determining the composition of the study, (2) computing the intermediate cost functions, and (3) combining these into the general function.

Since there is good reason to believe that public schools within a given state are subject to rather uniform influences on their abilities to raise operating revenues, public four-year colleges were selected as the basic elements in this model. Then it became obvious that the decision to use public four-year schools should be further delimited by studying schools within states as individual elements to reduce the influences of different money costs nationally for the same type of input, especially personnel. Comprehensive data for twenty-six states were obtained, and thirteen of these states were used, the remainder failing to meet preestablished criteria. The thirteen states that were used contained about 40 percent of all FTE students enrolled in this type of school in fall, 1967.

The intermediate cost functions for each state were calculated by fitting to per-student cost data both linear and parabolic functions by least-squares. In all cases the parabola explained more variance than did the linear function. Both original expectations and work by others suggested the superiority of the nonlinear function, and the model developed here bears out the premise.

Finally, the intermediate functions were used to estimate the coefficients for the independent variable (FTE students) when all influences on per-student costs, except the size of the school, are held constant. There is reason to expect some relationship between b and r^2 of a nature that is revealed when the two variables for the thirteen functions are studied. There was no reason to expect any correlation by definition, and a regression function for b on r^2 sets b at -0.244 when r^2 is unity.

The value of c should be related to b in a manner determined by the strength of the coincidence of the thirteen intermediate functions, either whole or in part, such as simply in the location of the vertical axis of symmetry. A linear regression function of c on b was shaped and located very much as would be expected, and this function was used to estimate c to be 0.00002275 when the previously determined b was −0.244.

Appendix C

A Review of the Literature

In Chapter 4 an attempt was made to develop a kind of nation-wide long-run average-cost curve for four-year colleges. The specific task has not been, to our knowledge, a very popular project for other writers. This appendix surveys the sparse body of literature concerned with the relationship between the size of institution and per-student educational costs. The first and most significant work examined is the study by John Dale Russell and Floyd W. Reeves for the North Central Association of Colleges and Secondary Schools. The other work here surveyed is the study of church-related liberal arts colleges by Reeves, Russell, and others.

The North Central Association Study

In 1929 the Commission on Institutions of Higher Education of the North Central Association of Colleges and Secondary Schools established the Committee on Revision of Standards to go about the task of "developing new criteria for the measurement of institutions."[1] A series of monographs entitled *The Evaluation of Higher Institutions*, reporting the findings of the special committees and staff, were published in the 1930s. The staff work for volume 7, *Finance*, was headed in the early days of the study by Floyd W. Reeves and was completed under the direction of John Dale Russell.[2] Today, owing to this work and others, these two men are generally recognized as the leading authorities on the subject of higher education finance.

1. L. D. Coffman, Foreword to *Finance*, by Russell and Reeves.
2. Russell and Reeves, *Finance*.

In a section of *Finance* entitled "The Relationship between Enrollment and Cost per Student," Russell and Reeves sought to establish a general relationship between the size of institution measured in student enrollments and educational expenditure per student. The data used for the determination of the general cost relationship were derived from an intensive study of forty-four public and private colleges and universities from across the nation.

Departing from an analysis and ranking of the quality or "excellence"[3] of each of the forty-four subject institutions, the authors sought to study the effect of the size of enrollment on educational expenditure per student, apart from any inter-correlation that might develop if the size of the institution and the quality were strongly correlated. (Their logic is that it would be expected almost without saying that quality and expenditure per student would have a strong positive correlation. Thus, if there *is* a strong correlation between the size and quality of the institutions, most certainly one will get a spurious correlation between the size of institution and expenditure per student. Ideally then, one should study a group of schools where there is little correlation between size and quality if he really wants to focus on the relationship between the size of instutition and expenditure per student.)

They were able to divide the forty-four schools into three rather homogeneous "excellence groups," and in two of these groups they found low correlation between the size of institution and the quality rating. These two groups of fifteen or sixteen

3. The "excellence" rating was basically a composite of subjective evaluations of all, and selected portions, of the schools' operations, combined with such objective measures as student body performance on standard tests in core subjects and apparent progress of graduate students (if any). The subjective evaluations of such things as the qualifications of the faculty, and the effectiveness of both the schools' general administration and student personnel services, seemed to play a dominant role in the composite rating. Ibid., pp. 114–27.

institutions served as the basic point of analysis; and, according to the authors, by this method of concentrating on groups of institutions with little correlation between size and quality, "quality is held constant or is ruled out of the picture by assembling groups in which quality is not an important variant."[4]

From this point, Russell and Reeves describe their methodology:

> A series of graphs were then drawn for each of these homogeneous quality groups. . . . The graphs showed enrollment on the vertical scale and one of the financial items on the horizontal scale. . . . Averages were also plotted for groups of from two to four institutions that were homogeneous in enrollment. A smooth curve-of-best-fit was then drawn so as to approach most nearly these average points and also to show the trend of points for the individual institutions.
>
> These curves all proved to be of the same general pattern, which may be described as a straight vertical line for enrollments of 1,000 students or more, and an approximation to a hyperbola for enrollments of less than 1,000.[5]

Figure C.1, a reproduction of the figure used by Russell and Reeves for illustrative purposes, will help clarify their statement quoted above.

One other noteworthy item is that Russell and Reeves's study was made in the early 1930s, and colleges and universities tended to be much smaller in those years than today. Recognizing that extrapolation is dangerous, the authors cautioned that "for enrollments larger than 3,500 the data of the present study are not entirely clear."[6]

Thus, Russell and Reeves collected expenditures and enrollments data on a number of institutions, identified two groups of schools that they felt were roughly of uniform quality and that

4. Ibid., p. 20.
5. Ibid., pp. 20–21.
6. Ibid., p. 36.

FIGURE C.1

Enrollment and Educational Expenditure per Student for Institutions in Lowest Quality Grouping

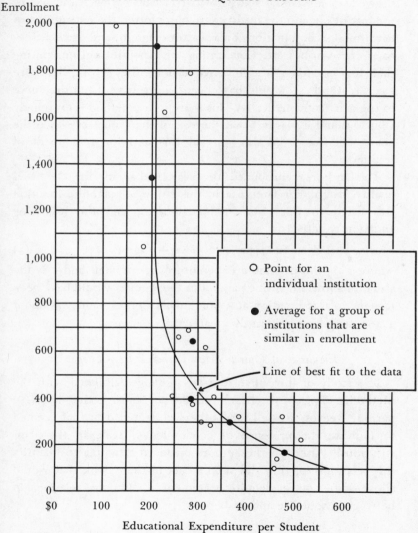

Educational Expenditure per Student

Source: Reprinted by permission of the publishers from *Finance*, vol. 7 of *The Evaluation of Higher Institutions*, by John Dale Russell and Floyd W. Reeves (Chicago: University of Chicago Press, 1935), p. 22. © 1935 by the University of Chicago.

showed no substantial statistical correlation between the size of the institution and the quality variable, plotted the expenditures-enrollments combinations on a scatter diagram, and drew a free-hand curve-of-best-fit. Concerning the possibility of computing their function in a more objective manner, they wrote, "A more exact method . . . would have been . . . to have fitted the curve to the data mathematically. This more exact method is extremely laborious and it was felt that the size of the group on which the curve was based did not warrant this extreme refinement of treatment."[7]

The authors reproduced the scatter diagram for the low-quality group. For later use in this study, a parabolic function was fitted to this data by least-squares, and the following equation resulted:

$$y' = \$487.50 - 0.384x + 0.000124x^2 \qquad (1)$$

where y' is the predicted expenditure per student and x is the size of institution. A line parallel to the abscissa would have been tangent to this function at a point where enrollment was about 1,800, a figure significantly greater than 1,000.

The Study of Church-Related Liberal Arts Colleges

In a study of thirty-five four-year colleges affiliated with the Methodist Episcopal church conducted during the 1928–30 period, Reeves, Russell, and others collected data that seemed to indicate the presence of economies of scale in these institutions.[8] Although the authors made no attempts to quantify this relationship, they did supply data in their book that would allow some more definite statement about the relationship between school size and costs.[9]

7. Ibid., p. 25.
8. Floyd W. Reeves et al., *The Liberal Arts College* (Chicago: University of Chicago Press, 1932).
9. Ibid., pp. 39, 492.

The thirty-five institutions were divided about equally between the accredited, of which there were seventeen, and the nonaccredited. Again for use in our study, rank coefficients of correlation were computed for the seventeen accredited schools, the rank-order approach being used because the schools were all in a very narrow size range except for a few relatively large institutions. Ascending ranks were assigned to the institutions proceeding from smallest to largest enrollments, while descending ranks were given to expenditures per student. That is, the ranks were assigned in such a way that a correlation coefficient of 1.0 would be obtained if the smallest school had the highest cost, if the second smallest school had the second highest cost, and so forth. Thus, a positive value for the rank coefficient of correlation will indicate a negative relationship between size of student body and costs per student.

When all seventeen institutions were ranked, the value for the rank correlation coefficient was .2998, certainly not a significant value for a sample of this size. However, the seventeen institutions were located all across the United States, and some variation in costs per student would have been expected because of regional differences in costs of inputs, especially faculty salaries.

So the seventeen institutions were divided into two groups based upon expected differences in factor costs owing to regional variation. The high-cost group included schools located in the upper midwest, the Middle Atlantic states, and California; the remaining six schools were placed in the low-cost group. The rationale was that higher factor costs could be expected in regions which have been characterized by industrialization and higher per capita incomes in the post–World War I period. It turned out that after this division of the schools was made, the rank correlation coefficient for the high-cost group was .5909, and for the low-cost group .7714. This crude attempt to remove the regional influences of factor prices resulted in, at minimum, a doubling of the measure of rank correlation. It appears that there definitely was some negative relationship between the number of students and per-student costs in this group of schools, once an adjustment could be made to eliminate the major source of variation in per-student costs other than size.

Summary

In this Appendix, the two most often cited works related to economies of scale in higher education were summarized. The most important was the study by Russell and Reeves for the North Central Association of Colleges and Secondary Schools. In the study, a group of institutions was selected on the basis of their rather uniform appearance of excellence, and little else. The schools were both public and private, and were located across the country. To the combinations of institution size and per-student costs, Russell and Reeves fitted a long-run cost curve by observation; this curve indicated that maximum economies of scale were realized by the time an institution had reached the 1,000-student mark, but the authors cautioned against attempts to make any conclusions on the basis of their work for institutions of more than 3,500 students.

The other study reviewed was also the work of Reeves and Russell, with associates; and the subjects were thirty-five four-year colleges with a common church affiliation. Although there were no attempts in the original work to quantify any relationship between the size of institution and costs, application of rank-order correlation methods to data from the study indicated a separation of institutions into accredited and nonaccredited groups, and further into high- and low-cost divisions based on regional location. The results were rather high rank correlation coefficients, indicating some negative relationship between the size of student body and per-student costs.

Appendix D

Miscellaneous Cross-Section Functions

This Appendix explores some efforts to compute cost relationships for activities within the total cost framework of state-supported four-year colleges, and fits statistical functions to cost data for state-supported junior colleges in two states. These approaches are not intended to be rigorous, but rather to complement the general function developed in Chapter 4.

Cost Functions for Educational and General Activities

Economic theory alone can do no more than logically construct the expected nature of the relationship between economic variables. The analysis of Chapter 3 suggested that total per-student costs in IHL, given some ceteris paribus assumptions, would decline as schools became larger, and then reach a range of constant costs. An econometric model of four-year colleges seemed to verify at least the declining cost range, and gave quantitative meaning to the function. The theoretical analysis of Chapter 3 concerning total costs was the sum of analysis about cost behavior for the separate activities within the broad educational and general budget. The object here is to study the behavior of these separate cost activities in much the same manner as total expenditures were studied in Chapter 4.

The fact that there is no settled state of production technology in higher education causes difficulties in any attempt to study the separate activities that make up total educational and general costs. For example, it appears that schools mix direct instruction and independent study in different ways. Such variations will influence the proportions of the budget devoted to instruction and departmental research and to libraries, respectively. Some institutions put more emphasis on the provision of nonacademic services to students than do others, which will also affect the distribution of funds among the educational and general activities. Some expenditure categories are more elastic than others. Finally, reported expenditures in the various budget accounts are subject to accounting vagaries. The point is that it would not be expected that analysis of *subexpenditures* within *total expenditures* would be as fruitful as analysis of the latter, especially in light of the influences discussed above.

It was possible to study instruction and departmental research; libraries; administration and general expense; and plant operation and maintenance for four of the six states with an index of correlation in excess of .8 for their intermediate function relating total per-student costs and FTE students. Each of these activities was reduced to per–FTE student costs for the schools in these four states, and a parabolic function was fitted by least-squares. The results are summarized in Table D.1.

We can make several observations about the data in Table D.1. First, as was noted in Chapter 3 (see p. 75) costs for instruction and departmental research should fairly well determine the trend of total costs; put another way, the size of an institution required to realize maximum economies of scale for instruction and departmental research costs should also be about the size that yields minimum per–FTE student total costs. Such appears to be the case in the real world, for we may see in Table D.1 that in states number 5 and 6 the minimum costs size for total costs and instruction and departmental research differed by not more than 300 students, while in state number 6 the difference was 1,200 students. However, it appeared that in state number 6 the rather inconsistent function for instruction and departmental research

TABLE D.1

INTERMEDIATE STATES, COST FUNCTIONS FOR SEPARATE ACTIVITIES: INDEX OF
DETERMINATION, CONSTANTS, AND MINIMUM COST LEVEL OF FTE STUDENTS

State Number	Index of Determination[a]	FTE Students, Minimum Costs	a	b	c
4					
Total costs	.6937	10,500	$2,061.23	−0.1690	0.000008050
Inst. and dept. res.	a	—	—	—	—
Libraries	.2383	43,200	99.95	−0.0049	0.000000057
Admin. and general	.4372	7,500	833.40	−0.2040	0.000013600
Plant op. and maint.	.4801	7,700	555.67	−0.1320	0.000008600
5					
Total costs	.9596	6,900	1,978.61	−0.2960	0.000021500
Inst. and dept. res.[b]	.8459	7,200	1,277.31	−0.1710	0.000011900
Libraries	b	—	—	—	—
Admin. and general	.5145	6,550	390.51	−0.0618	0.000004720
Plant op. and maint.	.7949	6,450	308.46	−0.0627	0.000004870
6					
Total costs	.9054	4,250	1,252.53	−0.2040	0.000024000
Inst. and dept. res.	.4346	3,050	610.55	−0.0706	0.000011600
Libraries	a	—	—	—	—
Admin. and general	.9661	3,900	319.82	−0.0939	0.000012000
Plant op. and maint.	.9997	7,250	251.14	−0.0481	0.000003320
9					
Total costs	.9294	5,400	1,266.16	−0.1450	0.000013400
Inst. and dept. res.	.1663	5,500	711.78	−0.0635	0.000005750
Libraries	.9867	5,900	131.78	−0.0227	0.000001930
Admin. and general	.9507	5,500	298.21	−0.0386	0.000003500
Plant op. and maint.	.7039	7,100	169.38	−0.0310	0.000002180

SOURCE: Computed from questionnaire data.

[a] Index of determination less than .1 is indicated by *a*.

[b] Inst. and dept. research includes libraries and organized activities.

expenditures was related to a mixed pattern of expenditures for libraries, and this was a state with few enough schools so that a "strange" mixture of expenditures between activities in only one school would significantly affect the derived functions for each activity.

Second, where the number of students was the dominant factor in determining costs per FTE student for the various activities, economies of scale were realized over a little wider range in activities other than instruction and departmental research. States number 6 and 9 best illustrate this tendency, which was alluded to theoretically in Chapter 3 (see p. 84).

Finally, the variation in the indices of determination within the thirteen states suggests that activities are influenced, in varying degrees, by considerations other than total students. Plant operation and maintenance seems most consistent in having a strong relationship to total FTE students, while instruction and departmental research costs are least sensitive to changes in total students. It may be that the former phenomenon is due to the tendency for plant operations and maintenance to be a kind of necessary evil to educators, with subsequent attempts to allocate only the necessary minimum to this activity. Also, the several state legislatures have been especially observant to ensure that any additional capital construction is justified by increased numbers of students, and it has been observed that the major influence on PM&O costs should be the size of the physical plant.[1] Thus, the legislatures have insured that the size of the physical plant is closely related to total students, while school administrators have ensured that the minimum amount is spent on any given physical plant. The result is that PM&O expenditures and total FTE students are closely related.

The reasons for an apparently weak statistical relationship

1. See above, p. 66.

between (1) instruction and departmental research and (2) total FTE students is less clear. One possible explanation might be that schools account for academic administration by charging either the instruction and departmental research account, or the general administration, general expense, and student services account. Especially when it is noted that it is common in small schools for the same person simultaneously to fill positions in both academic and general administration (for example, serving as both college business manager and chairman of the business department), some of the charges to instruction and departmental research might be arbitrary and differ somewhat among schools of essentially the same size. In short, there is a strong suspicion that the low statistical correlation between instruction and departmental research costs and total students is likely due more to accounting vagaries than to substantial differences in the actual allocation of inputs to direct instruction among schools of the same size.

Also, the low correlation between instruction and departmental research costs and total students that is exhibited in states number 6 and 9, at the same time that correlations are quite high for the other activities, might indicate that these other activities are allocated only a bare minimum that is necessary for some given number of students, and that whatever other monies are available are devoted to instruction. Since some noninstructional activities have higher threshold costs, and the costs are more fixed than others (and are, therefore, more or less elastic in relationship to total students), the amounts available for instruction might vary from an expected function to the extent that those allocating revenues to the schools do not recognize the different elasticities in cost functions for the noninstructional activities. That is, if decision makers overestimate the amount of funds necessary for a school to conduct activities other than instruction, given some number of FTE students, but are correct in their estimate of the amount required for instruction, given this same number of FTE students, the school could receive more in total than is required. Of course, the school spends this windfall, most likely in instruction. One or two instances of this in a cross section, involving either an over- or underestimate of the monies required for the noninstructional activities in the various-sized schools, will result in a quite mixed pattern of per-student expenditures in instruction and departmental research. Again, however, such a phenomenon is a product of short-run influences, and would not mean that instruction and departmental research per-student costs are insensitive to the number of total students.

In summary, the derivation of cost functions for the individual educational and general activities suggests they behave somewhat as the theory of such cost behavior would suggest. The shape of the function for total costs is most heavily influenced by the function for instruction and departmental research. The noninstructional activities are characterized by declining per-student costs over a little wider range of FTE students than for instruction, but by the time instruction costs have reached their per-student minimum, these additional declines in costs in the noninstructional activities are not of a large enough magnitude to have substantial influence on the trend of total costs. The derived functions for instruction and departmental research do not exhibit as close a relationship to total students as the theory developed in Chapter 3 suggested, but the reason is likely attributable to (1) short-run influences on the derived functions resulting from vagaries in accounting for instruction expenditures, (2) the effects of over- or underbudgeting the noninstructional activities in one year, and (3) both factors set against derived functions which contain only a few observations. There does not appear to be any evidence indicating that, in the long run, instruction and departmental research costs are relatively insensitive to the numbers of students.

Total Cost Functions for Junior Colleges

The junior colleges have been the recipients of much of the increased total enrollments in IHL in recent years, and the public junior colleges (especially the community college) have increased in numbers in recent years much faster than any other type of IHL.[2] These two-year schools differ from the four-year college more in degree than kind. Junior colleges provide the equivalent of lower-division courses, as well as many specialized types of vocational and adult education. On balance, one would expect the junior colleges to have real per-student costs only a little lower than those in four-year colleges of the same size because of the larger classes, higher student-teacher ratios, and less extensive library programs. However, the lower costs expected from higher student-teacher ratios may be somewhat offset by the greater concentration of vocational education programs, which typically make use of more academic hardware and have rather small classes. As concerns the other areas of expenditure, one would expect little difference between a four-year and junior college subject to the same kind of influences on their abilities to raise revenues.

The public junior colleges do not lend themselves to the extensive study that is possible with public four-year schools. Most states have adopted the community college concept whereby the junior college is an extension of the public school district, although typically with some financial assistance from state government. For these types of schools, however, the ability to raise operating revenue will differ a little intrastate because the overall financial position of the school district will play a crucial role. However, data were acquired on two states which have systems of state-supported junior colleges, rather than community colleges. Least-squares parabolic functions were fitted to their

2. See above, p. 23.

TABLE D.2

LEAST-SQUARES PARABOLIC FUNCTIONS: INDICES OF DETERMINATION AND CONSTANTS, TWO INTERMEDIATE STATES

State Number	Index of Deter- mination	a	b	c
5	.6029	$1,094.21	−0.150	0.000009540
8	.7188	1,231.82	−0.717	0.000186000

SOURCE: Computed from questionnaire data.

per–FTE student data in the same manner as for the four-year colleges, and the results are presented in Table D.2.

As would be expected, the long-run cost functions are quite similar to those of the four-year colleges, with the major differences being in the positions rather than the shape of the functions. State number 5 had a function for four-year schools which indicated that minimum per-student costs came in a school of about 6,900 FTE students; for their junior colleges, the low cost point was at about 7,900 students. For state number 8, the function for the junior colleges has a shape much like the function computed by Russell and Reeves, and may reflect more limited academic offerings in this state's system, as well as an extremely narrow range of institutional sizes, probably too narrow for a meaningful correlation.

The only significant discernible differences between the cost functions for two- and four-year schools is in the position, not shape, of the function. The difference will be such that a function for junior colleges will lie below that for four-year IHL in money terms. Partly it will reflect minor differences in real inputs per student; however, most of the difference is attributable to lower salaries in the junior colleges. Viewed in strictly real terms, the cost function for two-year schools will have a shape quite similar to that for four-year IHL, and the former will lie only slightly below the latter.

Summary

The theory of Chapter 3 concluded that costs per FTE student in four-year IHL should decline and then become constant, much in the manner of the firm of classical microeconomics. The attempt at empirical verification to support this theory seems successful. However, the theory for total costs represents the sum of theories concerning the behavior of costs for the separate educational and general activities, so these activities should also be studied.

There are some difficulties encountered when examining the costs of separate educational and general activities. No rigid production technology exists in contemporary higher education, and institutions have different philosophies concerning the proper combination of all activities into an educational experience. There are also short-run, as well as long-run, philosophical influences on the nature of such a combination. And accounting vagaries will result in financial records reflecting, with greater or lesser accuracy, the actual resources devoted to each activity during some time period. Finally, the different activities are student-elastic in various degrees according to numbers of students, and one should not expect the percentage distribution of total expenditures among all activities to be the same at every possible institutional size. Recognizing these limitations, least-squares parabolic cost functions were computed for the separate educational and general activities for four of the six states with the strongest correlation between total costs and FTE students.

The results of these correlations would tend to verify what was suggested theoretically in Chapter 3. The function for instruction and departmental research costs is most influential on the function for total costs. The noninstructional activities exhibit a tendency toward declining costs over a little wider range of school sizes than is true for instruction, but by the time the latter has reached least-cost enrollment, the additional economies of scale from the former are insignificant. The data suggest that the costs of instruction and departmental research are relatively little influenced (measured by the value of the index of determination between costs and FTE students) by the number of students, but the reason is likely due to accounting vagaries, especially in the allocation of some personnel expenditures among various activities. Another possibility is that occasions of over- or underbudgeting in the short term are mainly reflected in the expenditures for instruction and departmental research. In any event, there is no substantial evidence for a conclusion that total students is a minor influence on the costs of instruction.

The junior college is the fastest-growing type of American IHL today, but its study is complicated by the fact that most states have adopted the community college concept. In this type of system, the junior colleges are part of public school districts, and the finances of the two are closely related. However, two states with systems of state-supported junior colleges were studied, and the resulting cost functions relating total costs and FTE students are much the same as for four-year schools. The major difference between cost functions of four-year, as opposed to two-year, schools is that the functions for junior colleges will lie below those of four-year schools, although in real terms the difference is not as great as is the case when the data are unadjusted for differences in money costs of personnel. In all, there are no major differences between the microeconomics of four-year and junior colleges, as there is likely little difference between a cost function for universities, as opposed to the two- and four-year schools.

Bibliography

Arizona Board of Regents. *University of Arizona Financial Report for the Fiscal Year Ended June 30, 1968.* 1969.

Bain, Joe S. *Industrial Organization.* 2d ed. New York: John Wiley & Sons, 1968.

————. *Price Theory.* New York: Holt, Rinehart, & Winston, 1963.

Becker, Gary S. *Human Capital.* New York: National Bureau of Economic Research, 1964.

Brown, Roberta D. "Student Characteristics and Institutional Impact of the Large Publicly Controlled vs. the Small Private Institution." *College and University* 42, no. 3 (Spring 1967): 325–36.

California. *Traditional Detail for the Support and Local Assistance Budget for the Fiscal Year July 1, 1969 to June 30, 1970.* 1969.

California Coordinating Council for Higher Education. *Instructional Practices and Related Faculty Staffing in California Public Higher Education.* 1967.

California Legislature, 1967 Regular Session. *Analysis of the Budget Bill: Report of the Legislative Analyst to the Joint Legislative Budget Committee.* 1967.

California and Western Conference Cost and Statistical Study. Berkeley: University of California, n.d.

Cartter, Allan M. "Economics of the University." *Papers and Proceedings, 77th Annual Meeting, The American Economics Association* 55, no. 2 (1965): 481–94.

————. "The Economics of Higher Education." In *Contemporary Economic Issues,* ed. Neil W. Chamberlain, pp. 145–84. Homewood, Ill.: Richard D. Irwin, 1969.

Clark, Harold F. *Cost and Quality in Public Education.* Syracuse: Syracuse University Press, 1963.

Coombs, Philip H. "An Economist's Overview of Higher Education." In *Financing Higher Education: 1960–70,* ed. Dexter M. Keezer, pp. 12–34. New York: McGraw-Hill, 1959.

Coffman, L. D. Foreword to *The Evaluation of Higher Institutions. Vol. 7, Finance,* by John Dale Russell and Floyd W. Reeves, pp. v–ix. Chicago: University of Chicago Press, 1935.

Denison, Edward F. *The Sources of Economic Growth and the Alternatives before Us.* New York: Committee for Economic Development, 1962.

"The Economic Status of the Profession." *AAUP Bulletin* 54, no. 2 (June 1968): 182–241.

Edding, Friedrich. "Expenditures on Education: Statistics and Comments." In *The Economics of Education: Proceedings of a Conference Held by the International Economics Association*, eds. E. Austin G. Robinson and John E. Vaizey, pp. 24–70. New York: St. Martin's Press, 1966.

Georgia Board of Regents of the University System. *Annual Financial Report, University System of Georgia, For the Year Ended June 30, 1968*. 1969.

———. *Part I, Biennium Budget Request: General Operations, 1969–1971*. 1969.

Harris, Seymour E., ed. *Economic Aspects of Higher Education*. Paris: Organization for Economic Cooperation and Development, 1964.

———. "Financing of Higher Education: Broad Issues." In *Financing Higher Education: 1960–70*, ed. Dexter M. Keezer, pp. 35–78. New York: McGraw-Hill, 1959.

———, ed. *Higher Education in the United States: The Economic Problems*. Cambridge, Mass.: Harvard University Press, 1960.

———, ed. *Higher Education: Resources and Finance*. New York: McGraw-Hill, 1962.

Hirsch, Werner Z. "Expenditure Implications of Metropolitan Growth and Consolidation." *Review of Economics and Statistics* 41, no. 3 (August 1959): 232–41.

Illinois Board of Higher Education. *Fourth Biennial Report, 1967–1968*. 1969.

———. *Recommendations for Higher Education Operating Budgets, 1969–1971*. 1969.

———. *State-Wide Space Survey: Fall Term, 1965*. 1966.

Jencks, Christopher, and Riesman, David. *The Academic Revolution*. New York: Doubleday, 1968.

Kaysen, Carl. "Some General Observations on the Pricing of Higher Education." In *Higher Education in the United States: The Economic Problem*, ed. Seymour E. Harris, pp. 55–60. Cambridge, Mass.: Harvard University Press, 1960.

———. "The Corporation: How Much Power? What Scope?" In *The Corporation in Modern Society*, ed. Edward S. Mason, pp. 83–105. Cambridge, Mass.: Harvard University Press, 1961.

Keezer, Dexter M., ed. *Financing Higher Education: 1960–1970*. New York: McGraw-Hill, 1959.

Leftwich, Richard H. *The Price System and Resource Allocation*. rev. ed. New York: Holt, Rinehart, & Winston, 1960.

Lurie, Melvin. "Towards a Survey of Faculty-Turnover Rates." *Journal of Higher Education* 38, 7 (October 1966): 389–95.

Massachusetts. *Massachusetts Financial Report for the Fiscal Year Ended June 30, 1968*. 1969.

Miller, James L. *State Budgeting for Higher Education*. Ann Arbor: University of Michigan Institute of Public Administration, 1964.

Millett, John D. *The Staff Report of the Commission on Financing Higher Education: Financing Higher Education in the United States*. New York: Columbia University Press, 1952.

Mississippi Board of Trustees of Institutions of Higher Learning. *Analysis of Institutional Operating Budget Estimates for 1968–69*. 1968.

Missouri Commission on Higher Education. *Higher Education Statistical Report, 1968–69*. 1969.

——. *1969–70 Recommendations on Appropriations and Other Matters and 1967–68 Institutional Reports of Income and Expenditures and Report on Administration of Federal and Federally Related Programs*. 1968.

Montana University System, Office of the Executive Secretary. *Biennial Budget Presentation, 1969–71*. 1968.

——. *Report to the Montana State Board of Education, Ex Officio Regents of the Montana University System, 1967–68*. 1968.

National Committee on the Preparation of a Manual on College and University Business Administration. *College and University Business Administration*. Vol. 1. Washington, D.C.: American Council on Education, 1952.

National Federation of College and University Business Officers Association. *The Sixty College Study: A Second Look*. 1960.

National Industrial Conference Board. *Economic Almanac, 1967–1968*. New York: Macmillan, 1967.

National Science Foundation. *Geographic Distribution of Federal Funds for Research and Development: Fiscal Year 1965*. Washington, D.C.: GPO, 1967.

Nebraska. *Annual Fiscal Report, June 30, 1968*. 1969.

New Jersey. *Budget Message of Richard J. Hughes, Governor of New Jersey, for the Fiscal Year Ending June 30, 1970*. 1969.

North Dakota State Board of Higher Education. *Fifteenth Biennial Report of the State Board of Higher Education and the Institutions and Departments under Its Jurisdiction*. 1969.

Ohio Board of Regents. *Developments in Higher Education, State of Ohio, 1967–68: Fifth Annual Report of the Ohio Board of Regents*. 1969.

Ohles, John F. "Is the Laboratory School Worth Saving?" *Journal of Teacher Education* 18, no. 3 (Fall 1967): 304–7.

Oklahoma State Regents for Higher Education. *Current Operating Income and Expenditures: Oklahoma State Colleges and Universities, Fiscal Year 1967–68*. 1969.

Papi, Giuseppe V. "General Problems of the Economics of Education." In *The Economics of Education: Proceedings of a Conference Held by the International Economics Association*, eds. E. Austin G. Robinson and John E. Vaizey, pp. 3–23. New York: St. Martin's Press, 1966.

Pennsylvania Department of Public Instruction, Bureau of Statistics. *Our Colleges and Universities Today*. 1969.

Peterson, Richard E. *The Scope of Organized Student Protest in 1964–65*. Princeton, N.J.: Educational Testing Service, 1966.

Public Financing of Higher Education. New York: Tax Foundation Inc., 1966.

Ray, Gordon N. "Conflict and Cooperation." In *Financing Higher Education: 1960–70*, ed. Dexter M. Keezer, pp. 103–17. New York: McGraw-Hill, 1959.

Reeves, Floyd W.; Russell, John Dale; Gregg, H. C.; Brumbaugh, A. J.; and Blauch, L. E. *The Liberal Arts College*. Chicago: University of Chicago Press, 1932.

Rivlin, Alice M. "Research in the Economics of Higher Education: Progress and Problems." In *Economics of Higher Education*, ed. Selma J. Mushkin, pp. 357–83. Washington, D.C.: GPO, 1962.

Robinson, E. Austin G., and Vaizey, John E., eds. *The Economics of Education: Proceedings of a Conference Held by the International Economics Association*. New York: St. Martin's Press, 1966.

Russell, John Dale, and Doi, James I. "Analysis of Expenditures for Administrative and General Purposes." *College and University Business* 19, no. 6 (December 1955): 39–41.

———. "Analysis of Expenditures for Plant Operation and Maintenance." *College and University Business* 20, no. 2 (February 1956): 47–51.

Russell, John Dale, and Reeves, Floyd W. *Finance*. Vol. 7 of *The Evaluation of Higher Institutions*. Chicago: University of Chicago Press, 1935.

Schultz, Theordore W. "Capital Formation by Education." *Journal of Political Economy* 68, no. 6 (December 1960): 571–83.

———. *The Economic Value of Education*. New York: Columbia University Press, 1963.

Sliger, Bernard F. "Some Economic Aspects of Higher Education." *Educational Record* 42, no. 1 (January 1961): 62–66.

Smith, Adam. *An Inquiry into the Nature and Causes of the Wealth of Nations: Selections, Book 1*. Chicago: Henry Regnery Co., 1953.

South Dakota Board of Regents. *Operating Budget Recommendations, Fiscal Year 1970*. 1969.

Stigler, George J. "The Case against Big Business." In *Monopoly Power and Economic Performance*, ed. Edwin Mansfield, pp. 3–12. New York: Norton, 1964.

Stocks, Anthony H. *Considerations of Scale in Providing State and Local Public Goods*. Morgantown, W.Va.: Bureau of Business Research, 1968.

Thorp, Willard L. "Probabilities and Possibilities." In *Financing Higher*

Education: 1960–70, ed. Dexter M. Keezer, pp. 274–92. New York: McGraw-Hill, 1959.

U.S. Dept. of Commerce, Bureau of the Census. *Current Population Reports*. Series P-20, no. 169. Washington, D.C.: GPO.

———. *Statistical Abstract of the United States*. 1967; 1968. Washington, D.C.: GPO.

———, Office of Business Economics. *Survey of Current Business*. July 1968; July 1969; August 1969. Washington, D.C.: GPO.

———. *The National Income and Product Accounts of the United States, 1929–1965*. Washington, D.C.: GPO, 1967.

U.S. Dept. of HEW, Office of Education. *Biennial Survey of Education in the United States, 1956–58*. Washington, D.C.: GPO, 1960.

———. *Digest of Educational Statistics*. 1962; 1964; 1966; 1968. Washington, D.C.: GPO.

———. *Earned Degrees Conferred, 1965–66*. Washington, D.C.: GPO, 1968.

———. *Education Directory, 1968–1969. Part 3*. Washington, D.C.: GPO, 1969.

———. *Faculty and Other Professional Staff in Institutions of Higher Learning*. First Term 1961–62; Fall Term 1963–64. Washington, D.C.: GPO.

———. *Instructions for Completing OE Form 2300-4: Higher Education General Information Survey, Financial Statistics of Institutions of Higher Education*. Washington, D.C.: GPO, 1966.

———. *Library Statistics of Colleges and Universities*. 1963–64. Washington, D.C.: GPO, 1966.

———. *Numbers and Characteristics of Employees in Institutions of Higher Education, Fall 1966*. Washington, D.C.: GPO, 1969.

———. *Opening Fall Enrollments in Institutions of Higher Learning*. 1966; 1968. Washington, D.C.: GPO.

———. *Projections of Educational Statistics to 1977–78*. Washington, D.C.: GPO, 1968.

———. *Students Enrolled for Advanced Degrees, Fall 1967—Part A—Summary Data*. Washington, D.C.: GPO, 1968.

University of Colorado Office of Institutional Research. *Analysis of the Scope of Courses Taught, Class Size, Teaching Loads, and Instructional Salary Cost for the Regular Academic Year 1967–68 for Credit Classes at the University of Colorado: Boulder, Denver, and Colorado Springs Campuses*. 1969.

University of Nebraska Office of Institutional Research. *Analysis of Course Offerings, Class Size, and Teaching Load: First Semester, 1967–1968*. 1968.

Utah Coordinating Council of Higher Education. *Financing Higher Education in Utah, 1969–70*. 1969.

Virginia State Council of Higher Education. *Financing Virginia's Colleges: Current Operating Income and Expenditures, 1967–68.* 1969.

Watson, Donald S. *Price Theory and Its Uses.* Boston: Houghton Mifflin, 1963.

Wells, Harry L. *Higher Education Is Serious Business.* New York: Harper & Row, 1953.

Williams, Robert L. "Instructional Cost Studies in Perspective." *College and University Business* 26, no. 3 (March 1959): 28–29.

Wisconsin Coordinating Council for Higher Education. *1969–71 Coordinating Council for Higher Education Budget Recommendations for Public Higher Education in Wisconsin.* 1969.

Wolff, Robert P. "The Race for College." In *The Troubled Campus*, ed. by the editors of the *Atlantic*, pp. 124–35. Boston: Little, Brown, 1966.

Index

American Economics Association: address to by Cartter at 1964 annual meeting, 1

Auxiliary enterprises, cost accounting definition of, 58

Bain, Joe S.: on diseconomies of scale, 46; on economies of scale, 44–45; on least-cost combination assumption, 141–42; on social value of gigantic business firms, 125

Becker, Gary S.: on education as element in economic growth process, 3n

Brown, Roberta D.: on environmental impact of large versus small IHL, 125

Building space, interinstitutional comparisons of: problem of standard definitions, 66n

California and Western Conference Cost and Statistical Study: on per-student cost differences by discipline, 36

Cartter, Allan M.: on characteristics of universities, 30; on economists' interest in education, 1; on economists' neglect of microeconomics of higher education, 5, 7–10; on tuition differences in public versus private IHL, 121–22; on variations among disciplines in building space requirements, 67–68

Clark, Harold F.: on technological change in IHL, 31–32

College-ongoing rates, 19–20

Colleges and universities. *See* Higher learning, institutions of (IHL); Private IHL; Public IHL

Coombs, Philip H.: and first phase in study of macroeconomics of higher education, 4; on defects in capital markets for IHL, 128; on technological change in IHL, 32

Cost models: general administration, general expense, and student services, intermediate cost functions for, 166–68; general function, characteristics of intermediate functions in, 95–98; general function, common observations on implications for private IHL of, 119–22; general function, definition of full-time equivalent (FTE) student in, 146–47; general function, estimating coefficients for, 150–55; general function, influence of interinstitutional differences in abilities to raise revenue on, 90–91; general function, institutional composition of, 91–92, 144–46; general function, institutional size range in, 105–6; general function, mathematical description of, 98–104, 150; general function, planned maximum student-teacher ratio in, 93–94; general function, private

Cost models (*cont.*)

IHL's inability to realize economies of scale and implications of, 122–24; general function, rationale for gigantic multiversities and implications of, 124–29; general function, regression methodology for, 95–148; general function, relevance for private schools of, 107–12; general function, summer sessions cost accounting in, 147–48; general function, tests of significance for intermediate functions' coefficients in, 148–50; instruction and departmental research, intermediate cost functions for, 166–70 passim; junior colleges, analytical difficulties with cost functions for, 171; junior colleges, characteristics of intermediate cost functions for, 172–73; libraries, intermediate cost functions for, 166–68; plant operation and maintenance, intermediate cost functions for, 166–68; separate education and general activities, analytical difficulties with cost function for, 165–66. *See also* Russell, John Dale, and Doi, James I.

Costs, IHL: academic administration, theory of, 75–76; current total operating, 21, 37–40; current total operating, theory of, 83–84; direct instruction, differences in education and social sciences, 109; general administration, general expense, and student services (administration), theory of, 72–75; instruction and departmental research (instruction), theory of, 75–83; libraries, theory of, 70–71; organized activities relating to instruction, theory of, 71–72; organized research, 17–18; organized research, federal government role in, 17–18, 134; organized research and other sponsored programs, theory of, 133–36; plant maintenance and operation, theory of, 65–70; portion of total absorbed by core functions, 64–65n; portion of total absorbed by personnel, 55n; relation to geographic location of institution, 55–57; relation to revenue, 54–55; teaching personnel, theory of, 77–83

Denison, Edward F.: and second phase in study of macroeconomics of higher education, 5n; on education as element in economic growth process, 3n

Economic growth, education as element in, 2–3. *See also* Becker, Gary S.; Denison, Edward F., on education as element in economic growth process; Schultz, Theordore W., on education as element in the economic growth process

Economics of higher education, substance of, 3–4

"Economic Status of the Profession, The" (1968): on cost economies in public IHL, 122; on financial difficulties of private IHL, 119–20

Economists, recent attention paid education, 1–3. *See also* Cartter, Allan M., on economists' interest in education

Edding, Friedrich: on economists' neglect of the microeconomics of higher education, 11; on real depreciation of IHL, 99

Educational attainment: rural versus urban children, 19n

Education Directory, 1968–1969: on necessary criteria for identification as IHL, 12–13

Expenditures. *See* Costs

Extension and public service, cost accounting definition of, 59

Four-year college, characteristics of, 14

General administration, general expense, and student services (administration), cost accounting definition of, 60

Harris, Seymour E.: and first phase in study of macroeconomics of higher education, 4n; on below-cost pricing in IHL, 34; on student to staff ratios, 20

Higher education, definition of, 12–13

Higher education, economics of: definition, 2–3

Higher education, macroeconomics of: employment in, 15–17; enrollments, 18–20; first phase in study of, 4–5; indirect costs, 21–23; professional personnel in, 15–17; second phase in study of, 5. *See also* Coombs, Philip H., and first phase in study of macroeconomics of higher education; Denison, Edward F., and second phase in study of macroeconomics of higher

education; Harris, Seymour E., and first phase in study of macroeconomics of higher education; Keezer, Dexter M., on first phase in study of macroeconomics of higher education; Papi, Giuseppe V., on second phase in study of macroeconomics of higher education

Higher education, microeconomics of: below-cost pricing, 33–36; commodity price discrimination, 36; cost analysis, appropriate unit for, 52; economists' neglect of, 6–11; enrollments, 18–20; IHL, revenue for, 29–30; IHL, technological change in, 31–32, 49; inter-institutional competition, absence of, 53–54; manpower, production of own, 32–33; number, types, and growth of institutions, relation to, 23–24; output, measure of, 49–52; service versus product industry, 48–49; state government personnel, study by 6; statistics of, 36–40. *See also* Harris, Seymour E., on below-cost pricing in IHL; Papi, Giuseppe V., on below-cost pricing in IHL

Higher learning, institutions of (IHL): degree-mix in, 13–14; governance of, 13–14; revenue for, 38–40; size of, 24–28; variation in mixes of students and programs in, 141; variation in money prices for resources in, 142–43; variation of per-unit real costs, 140; variations in resource mix, 142–43. *See also* Clark, Harold F.; Coombs, Philip H., on technological change in IHL;

Higher learning, institutions of (IHL) (*cont.*)
Education Directory, 1968–1969; Ray, Gordon N., on decision making in IHL; Reeves, Floyd W. et al.; Russell, John Dale, and Reeves, Floyd W.

Instruction and departmental research (instruction), cost accounting definition of, 59

Junior colleges: definition of, 14; microeconomic characteristics of, 171

Kaysen, Carl: on characteristics of universities, 30–31; on social value of gigantic business firms, 125
Keezer, Dexter M.: on first phase in study of macroeconomics of higher education, 4n

Leftwich, Richard H.: on economies of scale, 45; on microeconomics, definition of, 44
Libraries, cost accounting definition of, 60
Lurie, Melvin: on economists' neglect of microeconomics of higher education, 6

Microeconomics: definition of, 44; diseconomies of scale, 46–47; economies of scale, 44–46. *See also* Leftwich, Richard H.; Smith, Adam
Miller, James L.: on state government budgeting for extension and public service costs, 137; on state

government budgeting for organized research costs, 134; on use of formulas in state budgeting for IHL, 141
Millett, John D.: on budgets for agricultural programs, 137; on hidden costs of departmental research, 135

North Central Association Study: comparison with general function, differences in level of threshold staffing, 118–19; comparison with general function, methodological differences, 116–18

Ohles, John F.: on demise of laboratory schools, 71–72
Organized activities relating to instruction, cost accounting definition of, 60
Organized research, cost accounting definition of, 60–61
Other sponsored programs, cost accounting definition of, 61

Papi, Giuseppe V.: on below-cost pricing in IHL, 34; on second phase in study of macroeconomics of higher education, 5
Peterson, Richard E.: on relationship between school size and scope of student demonstrations, 126
Physical plant maintenance and operation, cost accounting definition of, 60
Private IHL: donors, role in setting budget for, 30; establishing budgets in, 30; variation in abilities to

raise revenue in, 140. *See also* "Economic Status of the Profession, The" (1968), on financial difficulties of private IHL

Public IHL: coordinating boards, role in setting budget in, 29–30; governing boards, role in setting budget in, 29–30; governor, role in setting budget in, 29–30; legislature, role in setting budget in, 29–30; local school board, role in setting budget in, 30; property assessor, role in setting budget in, 30; variations in abilities to raise revenue in, 140. *See also* Miller, James L., on use of formulas in state budgeting for IHL

Rate, labor force participation: women, 22n

Ray, Gordon N.: on decision making in IHL, 25, 29

Reeves, Floyd W. et al.: and background study of church-related liberal arts colleges, 162

Regression models. *See* Cost models

Rivlin, Alice M.: on economists' neglect of microeconomics of higher education, 8–10

Russell, John Dale, and Doi, James I.: on general administration, general expense, and student services costs, theory of, 73; on plant maintenance and operation costs, theory of, 68–69

Russell, John Dale, and Reeves, Floyd W.: and background, North Central Association study, 158–59; and "excellence" ratings, North Central Association study, 159n;

and methodology, North Central Association study, 159–60; on minimum enrollment necessary for lowest per-student average cost, 117; and results, North Central Association study, 160–62

Schultz, Theordore W.: on education as element in the economic growth process, 3n; on indirect costs of higher education, 21–22

Sliger, Bernard F.: on economists' neglect of microeconomics of higher education, 7, 9–10

Smith, Adam: on economies of scale, 45

State-Wide Space Survey: Fall Term, 1965 (Illinois): on relationships between enrollments and size of physical plant, 66

Statistical analysis: cross-section approach, characteristics of, 89–90, 139–144

Stigler, George J.: on social value of gigantic business firms, 124

Student aid, cost accounting definition of, 58–59

Student-teacher ratio, planned maximum, 78–82

Student to staff ratios, actual, 20. *See also* Harris, Seymour E., on student to staff ratios

Theological school, characteristics of, 14

Thorp, Willard L.: on technological change in IHL, 32

Threshold staffing. *See* Student-teacher ratio, planned maximum

University, characteristics of, 14, 30–31. *See also* Cartter, Allan M., on characteristics of universities; Kaysen, Carl, on characteristics of universities.

Watson, Donald S.: on diseconomies of scale, 46–47

Williams, Robert L.: on appropriate unit for cost analysis of IHL, 52

Wolff, Robert P.: on the influences on college-ongoing rates, 20